WHAT MAKES GREAT MANAGERS GREAT

How to Raise Engagement,
Give Feedback, and Answer the
Questions No One's Asking

What
Makes
Great
Managers
Great

CURTISS MURPHY

HOUNDSTOOTH
PRESS

WHAT MAKES GREAT MANAGERS GREAT
*How to Raise Engagement, Give Feedback, and
Answer the Questions No One's Asking*

FIRST EDITION

ISBN   978-1-5445-4265-2   *Paperback*
       978-1-5445-4284-3   *Ebook*

Kayla,
For Gratitude

Jacob,
For Joy

Jenny,
For Love

Contents

Introduction

Were you prepared when you started managing people? Did you feel properly trained? I suspect not. Most managers wait five years for their first official training. Even then, the training is not that great.

Let me paint the picture of what probably happened. You were a strong employee, really good at your job. Next thing you know, you're a manager. And you've been waiting for proper training ever since.

If this sounds familiar, you already know that you can't wait any longer. Your employees are real people, with real lives. They deserve a great manager now, not in some distant future once "training becomes available." The time for waiting is over.

In *What Makes Great Managers Great*, I will share the five questions you need to be asking:

1. Do your employees know what's expected of them?
2. How do you give feedback?
3. What aren't your employees telling you?
4. Are your employees highly engaged?
5. What about low performers?

These questions matter. I will explain why. Then I will share the easy-to-use insights, tools, and rules that will help you answer them.

Some of what I share will defy conventional wisdom. Some of it may change how you think about your employees forever. All of it will make you a better manager today than you were yesterday.

I'm Curtiss, a vice president of engineering, a professor of game design, and most importantly, a people manager with thirty years of experience.

I spent decades mastering my craft. If you allow me, I will teach you how to clarify expectations, give great feedback, and discuss what's most important. I will teach you how to increase engagement, work with low performers, and use your influence to achieve results while maintaining trust.

Simply put, I will teach you what makes great managers great. Now turn the page, so we can get to it!

Part 1

DO YOUR EMPLOYEES KNOW WHAT'S EXPECTED OF THEM?

Chapter 1

Lack of Expectations

I'm an impatient person. I like to jump into things and get moving as fast as I can. So when it comes to teaching people management, my instinct is to skip ahead to the "good stuff."

Fortunately for you, this is not my first rodeo. I've learned there are some basics we just can't skip.

First, if you are reading this book, then you are almost certainly a leader. Yes, I'm serious. You are a leader. If you're not used to thinking of yourself in this way, don't worry. I'll define "leader" in just a moment, and it will make more sense.

Second, whether you are new to being a leader or have been leading people for decades, there is always more to learn. Your employees are unique, complex, and ever changing. Which means that *you* have to keep changing too. It's a critical part of your leadership journey.

Third, we need to define three terms: leader, people manager, and one-on-one. These are critical concepts that will be used throughout the book.

A leader uses *influence* to achieve *results* while maintaining *trust*. This simple definition focuses on three areas: influence, results, and trust. Being a leader has nothing to do with your title, how much money you make, or how many employees you have.

With this definition, it should be clear why I can say that you are already a leader. If you weren't, you wouldn't be reading this book.

> My definition of leader is inspired by the insights of two of the world's most-recognized leadership experts. Stephen M.R. Covey, author of the number one bestseller, The Speed of Trust, shares the insight that leadership requires results and trust. John Maxwell, a bestselling author with more than seventy published books, shares the insight that "Leadership is about influence, nothing more, nothing less" in *The Leadership Handbook*. I love these two insights. I love them even more when combined.

A people manager uses *influence* to help employees achieve *results* while maintaining *trust*. People managers are special types of leaders who focus on the employees within their purview. They have begun to shift their professional focus from themselves to others. That's why most of a people manager's work is accomplished through communication.

A one-on-one is an *employee-centric* meeting for discussing what's *most important*. The one-on-one is more than just a meeting between two people. It's the bread and butter of being a people manager.

In the book, *The Speed of Trust*, Stephen M.R. Covey explains that **trust** has four requirements:

- **Intentions**—having another's best interests at heart
- **Integrity**—being truthful, sincere, and authentic
- **Capabilities**—being able to walk the walk
- **Results**—cultivating a record of success

Great leaders (and great people managers) get results by having another's best interests at heart, acting with integrity, and being able to walk the walk. All of that builds trust.

Those were the basics that we couldn't skip. Now, on to the good stuff, or more appropriately, the *great* stuff.

WHAT MAKES GREAT MANAGERS GREAT?

Being a people manager is a huge responsibility. You have direct influence over other people's lives. It's not enough to just be okay at your job. The stakes are too high. You have to at least be good at your job, and even that is probably not enough.

So, what makes great managers great? That's the question I've been studying for almost three decades. It turns out the answer is quite simple.

Great managers ask the right questions, evaluate the answers, and work to become stronger today than yesterday. Then they do it again tomorrow. And the day after that. And the day after that, until one day, they look back and realize just how far they've come.

If you want to be a great manager yourself, then start by asking the right questions.

THE FIRST QUESTION: DO YOUR EMPLOYEES KNOW WHAT'S EXPECTED OF THEM?

The first of the five questions is the most important. To understand why, I'd like to introduce one of my employees, Sue.

Sue was a software engineer. She had a four-year degree in computer science and three years of professional experience. She wrote reliable code and knew every detail of her projects. Sue knew the history of old bugs, remembered the weird problems we'd encountered, and understood why the team had made important decisions. In my eyes, Sue was a strong performer.

Unfortunately, Sue was unhappy. She believed that I expected her to work more quickly, be more vocal in meetings, and focus less on obscure problems. She also believed that I expected her to tackle bigger projects. Worst of all, she believed that her peers did not value her work.

Sue was thinking about leaving.

Let's explore her thinking. First, Sue thought she knew what I expected of her. Second, she felt strongly that her peers expected her to do something else. Third, she had expectations of herself that didn't align with either her boss's or her peers'. She was confused, concerned, and conflicted. No wonder Sue was unhappy.

Sue, Chuck, and all the employees referenced in this book are not real people. Their stories are an amalgam of hundreds of experiences I've had over the years. This is true of all the stories involving other people. When I tell stories about myself or my family, the people are real, and the details are told as best as I can remember.

Sue's situation is not unique. In fact, this sort of disconnect happens all the time. To make sense of this, let's look at the Gallup Q12 survey.

Gallup is a research company that studies business performance. Over several decades, they interviewed millions of employees in seventy-six countries to determine which perceptions and behaviors could predict success. From this, they developed a simple, twelve-question survey called the Gallup Q12. Take a look at the first question on that survey:

"I know what is expected of me at work."

- Strongly agree
- Agree
- Neutral
- Disagree
- Strongly disagree

How would Sue have answered this question? Definitely not with "strongly agree."

Sue and I were not talking about what *I actually expected* of her. Nor were we talking about what *she actually wanted*. She was a strong performer, at risk for leaving, due to a lack of communication.

Like Sue, most employees are confused about what is expected of them. This is true across all levels of education, skill, and seniority.

Unless you discuss it openly, clearly, and precisely, your employees cannot possibly know what is expected of them. They can guess. They can make assumptions. They can infer. And they cannot know for sure.

This leads to confusion, disengagement, and poor performance that affects both the individual and the entire team.

WHY DON'T THEY JUST ASK?

Many managers assume their employees would ask for clarification if they were confused. Unfortunately, generally speaking, these managers are wrong. Most employees won't ask for clarification about what's expected of them.

We will explore why that's true later in the book. For now, just know that this holds true for just about everyone, from the most junior intern to the most senior executive. And it probably applies to your employees too. Which raises the obvious question: if your employees don't know what's expected of them, how can they be great at meeting those expectations? This is the first problem you must address if you want to become a great manager.

Fortunately, it's a solvable problem. In Chapter 2, I'll introduce the expectations activity. It takes about an hour. When you're finished, your employees will know exactly what's expected of them.

Chapter 2

Clarify Expectations

In the last chapter, I asked the first question: "Do your employees know what's expected of them at work?" As you just learned, the answer is probably "no." It might be "no" because you never told them, or because you or your employee are making assumptions. Either way, the answer is still "no."

My employee Sue didn't know what was expected of her. As it turned out, neither did I.

MY STORY

In the span of just twelve months, I'd had three different bosses. Each of them came from different backgrounds and with different perspectives. In that same time, the company had changed direction twice. My teams changed. My projects changed. The economy changed.

That's about the time I found myself sitting at a conference table with several other company leaders. I was lost in my thoughts. I flashed back to the first item on Gallup's Q12 Survey—"I know what's expected of me at work." With a great deal of angst, I realized that I had no idea what was expected of me.

If someone had asked for my answer right then, I would have answered "strongly disagree."

So, I decided to answer the question myself. I made a list of everything I *was* doing, everything I thought I was *supposed* to be doing, and everything I *wanted* to be doing at work.

I brainstormed a massive list. Then I organized the items into little groups. Next, I tried to capture the core essence of each group in a short phrase. I did this over and over until I had just four simple bullet points, which I reordered into the following list:

- Provide technical leadership for my teams.
- Cultivate psychologically safe, collaborative, and high-performing teams.
- Help others excel.
- Promote partnerships across the studio.

These were what I expected of myself, given my role in the company. I was pretty sure they covered what the studio expected of me. What I didn't know was if they captured what *my new boss* expected of me.

I gathered my courage, scheduled a meeting with my new boss, and explained what I was trying to do. I walked him through each of my four expectations. We discussed them, he asked for clarification, and after about twenty minutes, he said simply, "Okay. I approve."

After that, I knew exactly what was expected of me in any possible situation. New project? Random crisis? Employee challenge? As long as my approach aligned with my expectations, the answer was clear. I always knew which things I should focus on, where I should invest my energy, and what I was expected to do for my teams, my boss, and my company.

My engagement skyrocketed. My performance increased. The only difference was that I now knew what was expected of me.

I am a vice president of engineering for a mobile gaming company. I tell the stories that I know best. Don't worry if you aren't managing software engineers, quality assurance (QA), or artists. The tools, techniques, and insights can be used just as easily with employees in marketing, customer service, sales, healthcare, education, or with just about anyone doing non-trivial work.

FORMALIZING THE PROCESS

Since then, I've formalized the process for defining expectations. I've fleshed out each of the steps, iterated on the details dozens of times, and refined them until they could be used by anyone. Here's the short of it.

The expectations activity is a four-step process for clarifying your employees' expectations at work. The four steps create the mnemonic, BOSS:

1. **Brainstorm**—build a list of everything they do at work (twenty to thirty minutes).
2. **Organize**—move things around into groups of similar items (five to ten minutes).
3. **Shrink**—extract the core essence of each group in ten words or less (ten to fifteen minutes).
4. **Sacrifice test**—re-order the list until you wouldn't sacrifice something above for something below (five minutes).

Instead of a generic checklist with hundreds of items, you will define behaviors that are adaptable, unique, and easy to remember. You will increase your employees' engagement, multiply their strengths, and make sure they know exactly what's expected of them.

The expectations activity is an important first step to becoming a great manager, so let's walk through the four steps in detail.

Chapter 3

Expectations Activity— Brainstorm

The first step of the expectations activity is to brainstorm (the B in *BOSS*).

Ask your employee to brainstorm a list of short phrases that captures everything that's expected of them, by themselves, their peers, and you as their manager. Keep the focus from two weeks ago to about two months into the future. Capture the behaviors as sentence fragments that start with a verb.

This step usually starts out pretty well. When asked, most employees will highlight the things they are currently working on. For example, when I did this with Sue, she started out with this list:

- Write code.
- Implement the features.
- Commit the code to the repository.

- Double-check my code.
- Test my code.

Right away, I began to notice a problem. Sue's first five statements overlapped—a lot. They were all just variations of "write code." Sue was repeating herself.

You will probably see this with your employees too. In fact, it's common to all kinds of brainstorming for two reasons. First, there's **recency bias, which is the tendency to over-emphasize what's happened in the recent past**. Once Sue said, "write code," she became overly focused on that one idea.

Second, there's **functional fixedness, which means seeing only one purpose for an object**. Sue was sort of stuck on the idea that software engineers have only one purpose—to write code. When in reality, she does much more than that.

Fortunately, I'd seen this many times before with other employees. I had an easy fix.

I asked open-ended questions, such as "What *else* do you do?" The emphasis on "else" helped Sue to think more broadly. It also helped her realize that she does more than she thinks she does. Sue added a few additional items to the list:

- Help my peers solve problems.
- Share my knowledge.
- Give a presentation at the engineering roundtable.
- Participate in project planning.

That was a lot broader. Sue was now thinking about her peers, her growth as an engineer, and the various meetings that she attended. After asking, "What else?" a few more times, she also came up with these:

- Ensure my work is high quality.
- Learn our new tools.
- Be more efficient.
- Collaborate with the artists.

> For *mid-level* employees, the expectations activity may be the first time they've paused to think of their career as more than just a job. Asking them, "What else do you do?" will encourage them to think more deeply, helping them to realize they have a choice in how their journey unfolds.
>
> For *senior* employees, these sorts of questions can be a catalyst that helps push your strongest employees to the next level. It helps them grapple with questions such as "What unique value do I add?" and "How am I using my influence?"
>
> Clarifying expectations is good. Helping your employees ask powerful questions that empower them to take ownership of their careers—that's great!

At this point, the brainstorming step was going pretty well. Sue's list of expectations was beginning to cover more and more of her job. Plus, she was using language that was meaningful to her.

After a few minutes, Sue began running out of ideas. That's when I used the **rattle-off technique, which entails throwing out fifteen to twenty behaviors in rapid succession without pause or explanation**.

Here's how I did it with Sue:

> "There are a lot of other things you do. I'm going to list a whole bunch of them. Don't take notes, just listen for things that jump out at you: updating documents, prepping the builds, doing peer reviews, talking to the designers, coordinating with the producer, working with QA, meeting with the product owner, attending stand-ups, conducting interviews, onboarding new hires, fixing bugs, testing the app on different devices…"

The rattle-off technique has never failed me. It jumpstarts your employee's brain and clarifies what you're asking for, which should enable them to add a bunch of new items to their list.

Really strong performers will often forget to mention some of the most important aspects of their work. From their perspective, some things are so obvious and routine that they do them almost without thinking. These things will seem almost not worth mentioning, due to the curse of knowledge (also known as the curse of expertise). In reality, these are critical tasks, and you need to capture them. Keep asking, "What else?" or try the rattle-off technique to help them realize that you want everything, even the obvious stuff.

If you use the rattle-off technique, be careful not to take over the activity. You want your employee to *own* every item on their list, decide which are most important, and capture them in their own words.

In Sue's case, she added the following:

- Update the design document.
- Keep all documents in sync with the changing requirements.
- Help the artists get the art into the game.
- Ask for clarification from the designers.
- Ensure problematic bugs don't happen on other teams.
- Update our technical design documents.
- Keep on top of system changes.
- Learn how to write shaders.

After fifteen minutes of brainstorming, Sue had twenty-one items covering a broad range of expectations. While most employees generate a list of thirty to fifty items, twenty-one was enough for us to continue to the next step of the expectations activity.

Now that you've had a chance to see how the brainstorm step works, let's go over some ground rules.

GROUND RULE 1

You should capture the notes during the brainstorming step, not the employee. To show you why this matters, consider this story about Marcus, the product owner of the Alpha Team.

The Alpha Team was fifteen minutes into a complex discussion about an upcoming feature. It was a healthy, lively conversation being led by the product owner, Marcus. He sat at the front of the room, typing notes which were projected on the big monitor for everyone to see.

The arguments went back and forth; some were in favor of the new design, some against. As the conversation gained momentum, the ideas came faster and faster. And right at a pivotal moment, Marcus interrupted, "Hold on a second; let me capture this in my notes."

Conversation stopped. Fifteen people sat quietly, staring at Marcus. Soon, everyone's attention wandered to their phones and laptop screens.

Instead of guiding the creative process for the entire team, Marcus was taking notes. And because he couldn't keep up with the rapid-fire stream of ideas, he brought everything to a screeching halt.

You don't want this to happen during the expectations activity. So take the notes yourself. This will free your employee to focus on brainstorming without getting distracted by typos, grammar, or finding the perfect word.

> When I first began using the expectations activity, I let my employees take their own notes during the brainstorm step. I thought it might impart a greater sense of ownership over the content. Unfortunately, it never worked out. Every employee got stuck at least once on spelling, grammar, or phrasing. They stopped brainstorming. Nowadays, I always take the notes, and I tell them why right up front.

GROUND RULE 2

A great people manager *facilitates* the steps of the expectations activity while ensuring the employee *owns* the content.

Notice how I approached the brainstorm step with Sue. I asked open-ended questions, gave her time to think, and helped broaden her scope. When I used the rattle-off technique, I made sure that she continued to *own* the activity.

Sue defined the expectations, not me.

This is a vitally important concept that will take some getting used to. After all, your employees are going to add weird stuff to the list—sometimes it'll be out of scope, inappropriate for their job, or just plain wrong. You will probably feel compelled to make changes along the way.

Don't. You'll have a chance to fix all these problems during the organizing step. For now, just keep facilitating the brainstorming, capturing what your employee says.

GROUND RULE 3

The expectations should reflect the employee's uniqueness. Every employee is unique. They have specific areas of expertise, preferences about which kind of work they do, and solve different problems.

Even when their work is similar, each employee will describe it differently. One engineer's "robust code" is another engineer's "easily maintainable code." Both are capturing the idea of "high quality"—from their own unique perspectives. These phrases are not interchangeable. The words your employee chooses will convey subtleties that can have a profound impact on how they approach their work.

Of course, not all employees will describe their tasks with unique nuances like "robust" or "easily maintainable." In that case, encourage them to be more descriptive. For example, if Sue hadn't added more descriptive tasks later, I might have asked her what "write code" meant to her.

These nuances are essential to building high-performing teams; make sure you capture them.

GROUND RULE 4

Use precise language when facilitating the expectations activity. Through trial and error, I've discovered that the way I talk about the expectations activity impacts the success of the activity. Some phrases just work better than others. Over time, I've developed a script.

Try to develop your own script that matches your style. To help you along, here are some of the phrases that work for me:

- "Knowing what's expected of you is the number one predictor of employee engagement. And it turns out that most people have confusion about what's expected of them. Let's address that by walking through the expectations activity."
- "This activity usually takes about an hour; sometimes it requires two or three meetings."
- "Don't type. I will capture notes as best as I can. Your job is to think of everything you do. Once we have a list of thirty to fifty things, we'll organize them into groups."
- "When we're done, you'll have three or four behavior-oriented phrases that start with a verb."

- "To start us off, what do you think is expected of you—by me, your peers, and even yourself? This includes everything from two weeks ago to two months in the future."
- "Now that you see them laid out, how do you feel about your expectations?"
- "Expectations change over time. Let's revisit them in a couple months."

So far, we've walked through the brainstorm step of the expectations activity. We've explored open-ended questions, the rattle-off technique, and the four ground rules.

I used those techniques with Sue to create a list of twenty-one expectations in about twenty minutes. While Sue's list was unique to her, it was fairly typical of what I see. It was long and broad; used short phrases that start with verbs; and covered everything that was expected of her.

Sue's list was also typical in that it had several problems. First, the list was overwhelming—no one can remember twenty-one random items. Second, the list had redundancies, items that didn't belong, and items that were missing.

Let me show you what to do about these problems.

Chapter 4

Expectations Activity—Organize

Typically, the brainstorm step generates about thirty to fifty expectations. It'll generally include duplicates, need lots of refinement, and feel both overwhelming and unwieldy. That's as it should be—after all, you're asking your employee to list everything that's expected of them in their job.

When I did this with my own employee, Sue, she generated this list:

- Write the code for the game.
- Implement the features.
- Commit the code to the repository.
- Double-check my code.
- Test my code.
- Help my peers solve problems.
- Share my knowledge.
- Give a presentation at the engineering roundtable.

- Participate in the project planning.
- Ensure my work is high quality.
- Learn our new tools.
- Be more efficient.
- Collaborate with the artists.
- Update the design document.
- Update the documents whenever the requirements change.
- Help the artists get the art into the game.
- Ask for clarification from the designers.
- Ensure problematic bugs don't happen on other teams.
- Update our technical design documents.
- Keep on top of system changes.
- Learn how to write shaders.

With brainstorming done, Sue was ready to move to the second step—the O in *BOSS*—*organize* the list of expectations into three to five groups.

Work with your employee to group similar items together. Try not to overthink it—"good enough" is good enough. Just move one task at a time by asking simple questions, such as "Is this item related to these items over here?" Plan for this step to take about five to ten minutes.

As you organize the expectations, aim for three, four, or possibly five distinct groups. Less than three usually means the groups are too large or your employee hasn't covered everything they do. Six or more groups will make the final list less effective. I'll explain why in the next chapter.

During this process, most expectations will fall into one of five categories:

1. Core work
2. Collaboration, communication, and teamwork
3. Mentoring, coaching, and assisting others
4. Professional growth
5. Leadership

Knowing that most expectations will fall within one of these categories will make it easier to recognize the similarities between tasks. It will also help you facilitate this step more quickly.

Of course, these categories are guidelines, not requirements. You don't need employees to cover all five categories. Likewise, it's okay for employees to have multiple groups for a single category. For example, they might end up with two distinct groups that both fall under the core work category. Alternatively, they might lack any tasks related to leadership or mentoring.

I expect all my employees to continue growing professionally. It makes them stronger, which leads to stronger teams. It's a win for the employee, the company, and the customer. During the organize step, I keep an eye out for expectations that fit into the professional growth category. At the same time, I don't force it—sometimes the employee is focused on growth, sometimes they aren't. That's part of what makes them unique.

Sometimes you'll find expectations that don't seem to fit in anywhere. When that happens, just set them aside temporarily.

These stragglers will often find a home as you get further into the activity.

I worked with Sue for about ten minutes to organize her list of expectations. She created the following groups, in this order:

- Group 1
  - Help my peers solve problems.
  - Share my knowledge.
  - Give a presentation at the engineering roundtable.
  - Ensure problematic bugs don't happen on other teams.
  - Update our shared engineering documents.
  - Keep on top of system changes.
- Group 2
  - Write the code for the game.
  - Implement the features.
  - Commit the code to the repository.
  - Double-check my code.
  - Test my code.
  - Ensure my work is high quality.
- Group 3
  - Learn our new tools.
  - Be more efficient.
  - Learn how to write shaders.
- Group 4
  - Participate in the project planning.
  - Work with the artists.
  - Update the documents whenever the requirements change.
  - Help the artists get the art into the game.
  - Ask for clarification from the designers.

NEGOTIATE

Once you've got several groups of related expectations, it's time to pause. This will be your chance to fix the problems you noticed during the brainstorming step.

You are the people manager. While the employee *owns* the expectations, you have to *approve* them. Now's the time to use your influence to ensure that the final expectations are appropriate for this employee in their current role.

Specifically, you need to: add overlooked expectations, adjust scope (broaden or narrow), and remove inappropriate expectations.

Is it really a negotiation? Technically you're the boss. You could force any change you want. Of course, if you abuse your influence, you may cause your employee to question your intentions, motivations, and possibly even your integrity (a.k.a. the requirements for trust). So, be thoughtful, decide what's truly important, and use your influence selectively. In other words, yes, it's a negotiation.

ADD OVERLOOKED EXPECTATIONS

Sometimes, an employee might overlook something really important during the brainstorm step. Maybe they just forgot. Or maybe they didn't know it was expected of them. As their people manager, you need to account for this.

In Sue's example, I realized she'd forgotten to mention anything about Unity, the primary engineering tool she uses to build products. At that stage in her career, Sue had not quite mastered that tool, so I expected her to continue her learning.

After a quick discussion, we added one item to group 3.

- Become stronger in Unity.

ADJUST SCOPE (MORE NARROW OR MORE BROAD)

Sometimes, one or more expectations might be too broad in scope or too narrow. In either case, you need to negotiate with your employee to fix this.

In Sue's example, one of her expectations from group 1 read:

- *Ensure* problematic bugs *don't happen* on other teams.

As her people manager, I liked that she was thinking about this. At the same time, it was beyond the scope of what I expected of her.

Sue really couldn't *ensure* that problematic bugs don't happen on other teams. So I asked her some questions, clarified what was possible, and negotiated to adjust the scope. As a result, she changed her original wording to this:

- *Track* problematic bugs to *increase awareness.*

REMOVE INAPPROPRIATE EXPECTATIONS

Sometimes, an expectation falls completely outside an employee's purview. For example, a junior employee might include a task far beyond their skill level, or a senior employee might be taking on more than they can handle all at once.

A great example of this occurs in group 4 of Sue's list:

- Update the documents whenever the requirements change.

In our company, this task is expected of a designer or a producer, not a software engineer. Once I explained this to Sue, she removed the item from her list.

> Could you negotiate scope earlier, during the brainstorming phase?
>
> Some managers are tempted to negotiate each item after their employee says them. Other managers might want to tweak the scope themselves, as they are capturing the notes. Doing either will cause your employee to stop brainstorming. Be patient. Finish brainstorming, organize the list into groups, and then begin negotiations.

In this chapter, we walked through the organize step of the expectations activity. You learned how to group related items and negotiate to ensure their list matches your own expectations for this employee.

For Sue, I used my influence to add one expectation that had been overlooked, reduce the scope of a second, and remove a third that was outside of her purview.

After thirty minutes of brainstorming and organizing, Sue had a comprehensive list of what was expected of her, organized into four distinct groups. It was time well spent.

In the next step, Sue and I refined this long list into something concise, compelling, and easy to remember.

Chapter 5

Expectations Activity—Shrink

You've brainstormed with your employee. You've organized their list of thirty to fifty expectations into three to five groups. After some negotiation, you've accounted for everything that is expected of your employee, by you, their peers, and themselves.

And you still have a problem—the list is overwhelming, unwieldy, and impossible to remember.

The point of the expectations activity is to give your employees clarity, multiply their unique strengths, and increase their engagement. They need an easy way to know what they should and should not be focusing on so they can do their best work.

A list of fifty items isn't the answer.

SHRINKING THE LIST

Humans are limited by **working memory theory, which says the typical human brain can only hold four to seven ideas at one time (a.k.a. "slots")**. This is why we write things down when we go to the grocery store.

To make the big list easy to remember, you'll need to "**chunk it," or represent a whole bunch of information with something much simpler (for example, a word, phrase, or image)**.

Chunking is why phone numbers are broken into three pieces, like (555) 123-1234. Your brain remembers the three chunks separately—there's an area code, a group of three, and a group of four. Without the idea of chunking, most people would struggle to remember their own phone number.

Chunking is also why we invent mnemonics like BOSS. The single word helps you remember the four steps: brainstorm, organize, shrink, and sacrifice. Likewise, chunking your employees' expectations makes it easier for them to remember what's expected of them.

In the shrink step (the first S in *BOSS*), work with your employee to chunk each of the groups by distilling each one down into a short, behavior-oriented phrase.

Tackle one group at a time. Ask your employee which group they'd like to shrink first. Or start with the group that feels most like the employee's core work (such as writing code, creating art, or working with customers). Then shrink it down and move to the next group.

For clarity, if you had four groups before shrinking, you'd end up with four chunked phrases when you're done shrinking.

BACK TO SUE

Let's continue our case study of Sue. She didn't have a preference for which group to shrink first. So, I picked group 2, which described her core work as a software engineer.

- Group 2
    - Write the code for the game.
    - Implement the features.
    - Commit the code to the repository.
    - Double-check my code.
    - Test my code.
    - Ensure my work is high quality.

I asked Sue a series of probing questions: "What do these expectations have in common? How could you combine them? How would you summarize this group?"

These questions helped Sue identify the essence of each group. After some thoughtful discussion, she came up with a single statement:

- Write the code for the features in our games.

That was a good first attempt to shrink group 2. What was missing was some of the unique qualifiers from her original list. I asked her about the phrases "double-check," "test," and "high quality." Those felt unique to Sue. This led to her second iteration:

- Write the code for the features in our games, make sure they are high quality.

That's a pretty solid expectation. From there, we revisited the items in group 2 to make sure we didn't miss anything. She realized that this condensed chunk didn't explicitly address the item: "Commit the code to the repository."

After some discussion, Sue decided it was a minor detail implied by the phrase, "Write the code." She opted not to call attention to it explicitly. "Good enough" was good enough.

From there, it was time to refine the language until we had a clearly defined expectation in ten words or less.

As we learned earlier, the brain isn't great at remembering lots of information. So while Sue was able to shrink group 2 down to a single, behavior-oriented phrase, it still wasn't easy to remember. After some further refinement, Sue settled on this:

- Write quality code that helps create robust games.

Sue had chunked her core work down to eight simple words. Fantastic!

WASH, RINSE, AND REPEAT

After shrinking group 2, we repeated the process for groups 1, 3, and 4. When we were finished, Sue's expectations looked like this:

1. Collaborate effectively with the artists and designers.
2. Write quality code that helps create robust games.
3. Become a stronger Unity engineer.
4. Share my expertise to help my peers.

Each phrase was clear, concise, and unique to Sue. Each began with a verb.

Viewed together, these four statements covered everything expected of her as a software engineer. Plus, they reflected what Sue expected of herself and what I expected of Sue.

At the start of the shrink step, Sue was overwhelmed. She was unsure how that gigantic list of expectations would be helpful.

By the end of the shrink phase, her tone had changed completely. Sue was excited, confident, and engaged. She was proud of her new list. She felt a strong sense of ownership. She felt empowered.

We were almost done. The final step involved ordering the expectations to ensure she wouldn't sacrifice what's most important.

Chapter 6

Expectations Activity—Sacrifice

The final step of the expectations activity is the sacrifice test (the second S in *BOSS*): order the refined expectations such that the employee would not *sacrifice* the expectations above for those below; the core work usually ranks first.

This step is relatively simple. At the same time, it can be difficult for some employees to understand what it means to prioritize one expectation over another. I use the word "sacrifice" because it helps them understand *how* to prioritize.

BACK TO SUE

At the start of the sacrifice test, I asked Sue how she would order her expectations.

> Sue said, "I think collaboration has to go first. How can I be effective if I don't have good relationships with my peers?"

I said, "Fair enough. Let's look at this a different way. Would you *sacrifice* writing quality code to collaborate effectively with your peers?"

"Oh, no. I get it. Writing quality code is definitely a higher priority."

In my experience, most employees are like Sue. Once they hear the word "sacrifice," the proper order becomes self-evident. For example, few employees would sacrifice their core work for anything else, which is why the core work usually rises to the top of the list.

In Sue's case, she reordered her expectations as follows:

1. Write quality code that helps create robust games.
2. Collaborate effectively with the artists and designers.
3. Share my expertise to help my peers.
4. Become a stronger Unity engineer.

To get to this final order, Sue realized that she would not sacrifice "write quality code" to "collaborate effectively." Similarly, she would not sacrifice "share my expertise" to "become a stronger Unity engineer." After she figured that out, the list practically sorted itself.

She was happy; I was happy.

Typically, reordering expectations only takes a few minutes unless the employee is going through a significant growth phase, is quite junior, or is a low performer.

As a final thought, note that Sue's expectations covered four of the five categories we introduced in the organize chapter.

1. Write quality code that helps create robust games (core work).
2. Collaborate effectively with the artists and designers (collaboration).
3. Share my expertise to help my peers (mentoring).
4. Become a stronger Unity engineer (professional growth).

Also note that they were in the default order. In my experience, that is pretty typical. It's why I listed the categories the way I did. Of course, not everyone will follow that pattern. After all, each employee is unique.

Don't worry about covering all five categories. And don't force your employees' expectations to follow the same order as Sue's. Their order should make sense for where they are along their professional journey.

For example, new hires, transfers, and employees undergoing a significant shift in responsibility might put learning first (i.e., professional growth). Or, they might start with the expectation to meet their teammates (i.e., collaboration).

That said, most employees will end up with their core work first. After all, that's generally what they were hired to do.

Back in Chapter 1, we learned that Sue was a strong software engineer who was unhappy at work. There was a serious disconnect between what I expected and what Sue *thought* I expected.

Together, Sue and I completed the four steps of the expectations activity. She then had a clear, concise list describing what was expected of her by herself, her peers, and me as her manager.

Sue left our meeting feeling confident, empowered, and focused on what mattered most. Over the coming weeks and months, Sue thrived. With just one hour of thoughtful discussion, Sue went from a frustrated, unhappy flight risk to a thriving employee who was deeply engaged with her work!

This is what it means to use influence to achieve results while maintaining trust.

Before we wrap up, there are a few extra things to know about the expectations activity, such as *What do you do with new hires? What are the special challenges with senior employees? And what about expectations for yourself?*

Chapter 7

Expectations Activity— Final Thoughts

The expectations activity is one the most important things you can do in your one-on-ones. It ensures your employee knows exactly what's expected of them, which leads to greater engagement. That, in turn, benefits your team, company, and customers.

Now that you understand the fundamentals of the expectations activity, let's highlight five additional considerations:

1. New hires
2. Senior employees
3. Timeliness and relevance
4. Walk the walk
5. Limitations of the expectations activity

1. NEW HIRES

Meet Chuck. Chuck demonstrated extensive knowledge, passion, and a hunger for learning during his interview at our studio. He sat in my office on his very first day, looking both scared and excited. I opened his first one-on-one with these words:

> "You've spent weeks learning about our company, interviewed with ten different people, and spent several weeks thinking about your new job while waiting for today. Now that you're here, *what do you think is expected of you—by your peers, me, and yourself over the next two months?*"

Not surprisingly, Chuck had a lot of ideas. Together, we walked through the four steps of the expectations activity. After forty-five minutes, Chuck had distilled a unique set of expectations, tailored to his level of experience:

- Ramp up quickly so I can contribute.
- Become a strong, professional engineer.
- Communicate with others to understand the problems.

These action-oriented, concise phrases encompassed everything that was expected of Chuck at work. He began his new career with a sense of clarity, feeling empowered and engaged.

I almost always do the expectations activity with new hires on their very first day.

New hires have been thinking about their new job for weeks, sometimes months. The expectations activity builds a bridge between your expectations and theirs. It's the perfect way to set them up for long-term success!

2. SENIOR EMPLOYEES

The four steps (BOSS) of the expectations activity usually go smoothly with junior employees like Chuck. Ironically, the same is not always true for more experienced staff. In fact, the more senior an employee is, the longer it can take, particularly during the shrink step.

Experienced employees have developed nuanced motivations about how they approach their work. While these motivations impact just about everything they do, they probably haven't given them much thought. And they most likely have never tried to explain those motivations to someone else.

Senior employees often need more time to sort this out. And by more time, I mean days, or even weeks! This is actually a good thing.

At the same time, my experience has shown that it's better to end up with a draft version of expectations than it is to end up with multiple, half-finished steps. So try to get through all four steps (BOSS) in a single one-on-one, even if it means putting a pin in various items, treating the list as a draft, and continuing the discussion later.

After all, you're going to revisit the expectations again soon enough.

An MMO is a massively multiplayer online game that costs hundreds of millions of dollars to develop. People who play these games are loyal, often logging thousands of hours of game time over years, even decades. These players pay a monthly premium to access new content each time they log in. Without new content, valuable players lose interest and eventually quit. This is why the MMO industry has the expression: content is king.

Strong employees are a bit like loyal MMO players. They are devoted, have years of experience, and constantly require new content. For employees, "new content" means new challenges, new things to learn, and new opportunities to become even stronger.

Done well, the expectations activity creates meaningful content for your strongest employees. It pushes them to take ownership of their careers, go beyond where they are now, and strive to become even stronger. If your employee is invested enough to spend days or even weeks exploring their expectations, then that creates wonderful new content for them. And that's a win for everyone.

3. TIMELINESS AND RELEVANCE

As the axiom goes, "Change is the only constant." Companies change. Bosses change. The day-to-day work changes. And most importantly, your employees change. They learn new skills, increase their influence, and generally become stronger employees.

To account for this, revisit the expectations activity whenever something changes with your employees (e.g., promotion, team change, role change, etc.). If the change was massive, revisit them again in about six to eight weeks. In the rare case that nothing is changing, review them periodically (e.g., twice a year).

To see this in practice, let's revisit my personal expectations from Chapter 2 to see how I updated them after a change:

1. Provide technical leadership for my teams.
2. Cultivate psychologically safe, collaborative, and high-performing teams.
3. Help others excel.
4. Promote partnerships across the studio.

My boss had approved those expectations. Unfortunately, not long after that, he quit. Then I got a new boss, and later, a promotion. My purview expanded to include the art department and two more teams. Then came the Covid shutdown, and our studio went remote. After all these changes, it was past time to revisit my own expectations.

Of my four expectations, surprisingly, the first three were still relevant. After we switched to remote work, my fourth expectation just wasn't practical. I began brainstorming new expectations that were not covered by items 1, 2, and 3 above:

- Learn new techniques.
- Continue reading books.
- Stay abreast of current trends.
- Read articles about people leaving the industry.
- Learn better ways to increase engagement.
- Codify my theories (less vague).
- Evolve my ideas through additional practice.
- Find better ways to teach what I know.
- Look for stories that fit.
- Bring compelling topics to team one-on-ones.
- Ensure all hires are thriving.

- Figure out how to solve team drift while working hybrid.
- Create new initiatives for a thriving, hybrid workforce.

First, note that "promote partnerships" didn't appear in my new list. Second, note that the five statements at the top were very similar—recency bias in action.

After brainstorming, I skipped organizing, heading straight to the shrink phase. Two words jumped out immediately: "hybrid" and "thriving." These were critical new aspects of how I thought about my work. Here was my first attempt to shrink:

- Combination of me learning/growing—with the aim of building a thriving, hybrid workforce

That wasn't a behavior; it didn't even start with a verb. After further reflection, something more powerful emerged:

- Rise to the challenges of a hybrid workforce.

When I presented this last statement to my new boss, she didn't like that I'd dropped the idea of "promoting partnerships" from my previous expectations, so I made one final change:

- Rise to the challenges of a hybrid studio.

The word "studio" included more than just the employees in my own "workforce." My boss loved the change. Negotiation complete. Expectations updated, relevant, and approved!

The brainstorm and shrink steps are the perfect combo for

updating a single expectation. The other steps can also be mixed and matched, as needed.

4. WALK THE WALK

At this point, you should have a solid understanding of how the expectations activity works. Now, it's time to put what you've learned into practice.

Do the expectations activity by yourself, for yourself. Complete all four steps, start to finish. This will give you a better understanding of how each step works. It will also give you greater clarity about what is expected of *you* at work.

Plus, doing the expectations activity for yourself will encourage you to figure out what you are trying to accomplish as a leader. This is known as a **leadership statement—the big-picture results you're hoping to achieve with your influence**.

In my experience, most managers haven't spent much time thinking about what it is they themselves are trying to achieve. As a result, they let the crises of the day dictate their actions as a leader. If this sounds familiar, now is the time to take charge of your own leadership journey.

Think about what you want to accomplish. Then include that in your brainstorming and ensure it's uniquely captured in your final expectations.

To see what this looks like in practice, refer back to my second expectation: "Cultivate psychologically safe, collaborative, and high-performing teams." That statement calls out what's most important to me, ensures that I am doing what truly matters, and helps me navigate the truly difficult moments of being a people manager.

Once you've defined *what* you're trying to achieve, consider going a bit deeper to uncover your **"why"—the deep personal motivation for doing what you do**. This is an advanced concept that becomes more important the further you advance as a leader.

To see what a "why" looks like, refer back to my third expectation: *"Help others excel."* That's the reason that I taught company-wide people management workshops, became a professor, and wrote this book. If you're not quite ready to define *why* you want to be a leader, at least try to capture what you are trying to achieve with your influence.

Doing the expectations activity for yourself will make you a stronger people manager, even if you never share it with anyone else.

Simon Sinek introduced the world to the **Golden Circle**. This is the idea that great leaders don't start by asking "What" or "How." Great leaders start by asking "Why." The Golden Circle is a simple, powerful idea that changed the way I lead my teams. If you want to know why it's a circle, check out Sinek's talk, "How Great Leaders Inspire Action." It is one of the top five most-watched Ted Talks for a reason.

5. LIMITATIONS OF THE EXPECTATIONS ACTIVITY

Now that you know how to use the expectations activity, let's pause to ensure you don't misuse it.

The expectations activity is not like quarterly objectives, ninety-day checklists, or yearly goals. The expectations activity is unconventional—it has a different purpose, is generated differently, and results in a different kind of list.

These differences come with serious limitations you must respect.

Difference	Benefit	Limitation
Expectations evolve frequently.	Supports employee growth. Adapts to changes in role, project, or organization.	Expectations are constantly shifting, making them inappropriate for measuring performance.
Expectations are behaviors, not outcomes.	Pushes the employee to perform continuously. Promotes long-term engagement.	Expectations cannot be completed, "checked off," or part of a specific, measurable, achievable, realistic, and time-bound (SMART) goal.
Expectations are unique to the individual.	Empowers the employee; increases clarity about their unique role.	Unique expectations cannot be standardized between employees, departments, or job titles.

The expectations activity results in ever-changing expectations that are unique to each individual. This leads to a critical rule.

Never use an employee's performance in the context of the expectations activity to justify a promotion, raise, or employee rating. I cannot overstate how important this is.

Using the expectations activity for job title-related advancement is fundamentally wrong. Doing so would involve both a misunderstanding and a misapplication of everything it is designed to achieve.

The expectations activity addresses the question, "Do my employees know what's expected of them?" You're going to need different tools to measure an employee's performance. We'll explore those tools when we ask the questions, "How do you give feedback?" and "What about low performers?"

Do you know what's expected of you at work? Use the four steps (BOSS) of the expectations activity to make sure you do. Then do the same with each of your employees. Define crystal-clear expectations, increase engagement, and empower your employees to focus on what's most important.

The expectations activity is one of the best ways to use your influence to achieve amazing results while maintaining trust. The more you do it, the simpler it will become. Eventually, you will have a hard time imagining being a people manager without it.

Of course, clarifying expectations is only the beginning. Your employees also need guidance, mentorship, and above all, feedback. That leads us to our second question.

Part 2

HOW DO YOU
GIVE FEEDBACK?

Chapter 8

Tools for Feedback

As I said before, I'm impatient. So, while I am personally very interested in the science of feedback, that's not where I want to start with our second question. This time, we'll skip ahead to the good stuff.

I spent decades studying how to give great feedback. I tried dozens of techniques, worked with hundreds of employees, and eventually, discovered some unconventional answers.

In this section, I'm going to share what I learned. Some of it is quite radical. Some of it will change the way you think about your employees forever. All of it is grounded in a basic definition.

From the people manager's perspective, **feedback is a collection of *tools* used to achieve *results* related to an employee's performance.**

This is not a complicated idea. You need *tools* for giving feedback, and you want *results*, as in, an improvement in your employees' performance. With this simple definition in mind, I am going to say something radical.

There are only five feedback scenarios:

1. Your employee is *confused.*
2. Your employee *lacks knowledge/skill.*
3. Your employee is *disengaged.*
4. Your employee is (or is becoming) a *low performer.*
5. Your employee is a *strong performer.*

That's it, just those five. To be crystal clear, allow me to say this in stronger terms. Every possible reason for a people manager to give feedback to an employee fits within one of these five scenarios. Period.

Let's explore them one by one.

1. YOUR EMPLOYEE IS CONFUSED

In the first scenario, your employee is confused about some aspect of the work. This happens every single day, in almost every company—pretty much any time there is a change in people, direction, or work that involves more than two people.

Confusion is especially prevalent when the work is dynamic, creative, or requires adaptation to unique situations.

Employees get confused about lots of things, from the tiniest detail all the way to the big-picture vision. They get confused when the work is new, when the process changes, or when new information arrives.

Whatever the reason, the outcome is the same. Confusion is common, and it almost always affects performance. As the people manager, it's your job to figure out when your employees are confused. It's also your job to remove the confusion as soon as possible.

Here are some great feedback tools to use when your employee is confused.

Tools for Individuals	How to Use	When to Use
The expectations activity	The expectations activity removes confusion at the macro level. It promotes long-term engagement, growth, and high performance.	Use this when an employee's role, team, or long-term work changes; also periodically.
"Not-just-any-rock" (see below)	If you need something specific, then provide a detailed, thorough description. Even better, provide a concrete example (a picture is worth a thousand words).	Use this when the work is unexpected, time is of the essence, or you think that confusion is likely to occur.
Check for understanding	This is our bread-and-butter tool for removing confusion. Ask the employee to restate their understanding in their own words (i.e., "reflection"). Ask probing questions that expose confusion. Ask, "What thoughts, questions, or concerns do you have?"	Use this when assigning new work to an individual or when an employee isn't performing well on a task.

Tools for Teams	How to Use	When to Use
Slow down to speed up	Pause the work. Bring everyone together. Walk through the details. Give every individual a chance to speak, raise concerns, and ask questions.	Use this when a team is pivoting, information is dynamic, or time is critical (the tighter the deadline, the more important it is to pause).
Recap	Have someone recap the decision, including all details. If questions or discussion follows, start the recap over with a different person. Recaps should be done by the person with either the lowest status or the least knowledge—this increases the odds that someone else will offer corrections.	Use this when a decision is being made that affects more than two people.

In the above table, I used the expression "not-just-any-rock." I originally learned what this means while developing training games for the military.

The general says, "Private! Bring me a rock."

When the private returns with a rock, the general says, "No, I need a round rock."

The next time, the general says, "No, smaller, something I can hold."

"With flecks of quartz."

"Smoother."

The lesson of the story is that leaders are often the source of confusion. And, while it seems silly in the context of asking for a rock, this is common in business settings. It happens most often when a leader needs something quickly or when the leader isn't crystal clear about exactly what they need. Before you know it, they've sent an employee to "bring me a rock."

Not-just-any-rock means providing clear, concise, explicit instructions, preferably with an example, especially when the work is new, unexpected, or urgent.

Good people managers try not to be the source of confusion. Great people managers know that confusion is common, so they work actively to remove it. It's one of the easiest ways to improve both individual and team performance.

2. YOUR EMPLOYEE LACKS KNOWLEDGE/SKILL

Once you're certain your employees are not confused, the next scenario to consider is that they lack either the knowledge or the skill to perform a specific task.

This is especially common with new hires and junior employees. Most companies and people managers plan for this by creating onboarding plans, defining initial goals, and establishing mentorship programs.

Less commonly, this can happen when we ask mid-level and senior employees to do something outside of their usual role. Because these employees are good at *some* tasks, it's easy to fall into the trap of assuming they will be good at *all* tasks.

Here are some great feedback tools to use when your employee lacks knowledge/skill.

Tools	How to Use	When to Use
Assess gaps in knowledge or skill	Ask the employee to explain what they already know, demonstrate the skill, or explain how they will tackle the problem.	Use this when assigning a new type of work or when an employee appears to be struggling.
Teach the employee	Teach them how to do the work. Be specific, be patient, and provide opportunities to practice. Assign a mentor, coach, or partner (as needed). Use active listening skills to confirm understanding and learning (see Part 3).	Use this when you've already identified a gap in knowledge or skill.
Check in frequently	Schedule check-ins. Engage frequently to follow their progress. Periodically reassess their knowledge/skill.	Use this when you've previously identified a gap in knowledge or skill.
Adopt the correct leadership style (see below)	Use situational leadership to switch between the four styles of leadership: directing, coaching, supporting, and empowering.	Use this with all employees, at all times.

In the above table, I introduced a new term. *Situational leadership* **means the people manager intentionally switches among four styles of leadership, based on the level of the employee's knowledge/skill**.

- **Directing**—when the employee's skill/knowledge is limited, the people manager gives precise direction, with frequent check-ins, clear examples, and lots of teaching.
- **Coaching**—once the employee has some skill/knowledge, the people manager shifts to coaching. The best tool for coaching is to ask meaningful questions that promote

learning. For example, "How did it go?" "What would you do differently next time?" and "Would you like ideas for making this even stronger?"

- **Supporting**—once the employee has proven performance, the people manager can assume a support role. Facilitate further growth with questions like "How can I help you to succeed?"
- **Empowering**—when the employee has mastered the knowledge/skill, the people manager only needs to share their vision for what should be accomplished before giving the employee autonomy over the execution.

My younger self used to say, "I *always* empower my strong employees." Years later I realized that my thinking was naive, myopic, and wrong. I missed the fact that a strong employee isn't equally strong at everything.

Sometimes, even my strongest employees need me to revert back to supporting, or coaching, or even directing. Over time, I learned to pivot among the four styles in real time.

Listen to your employees. Try to discern where they are thriving and where they aren't. Change your leadership style based on their current needs. If you aren't sure which style to use, consider just asking your employee, "What kind of feedback would you like?"

> It's deceptively easy to assume that your best employees know everything about everything. To combat this type of bias, try to remember that everyone has at least one skill that requires each of the four levels of situational leadership. And when I say everyone, I mean everyone, including you and me.

3. YOUR EMPLOYEE IS DISENGAGED

If you've already accounted for the possibility that your employee is confused or lacks knowledge/skill, then they might be drifting into more dangerous territory. The third feedback scenario occurs when your employee has become disengaged from the work.

Maybe they are bored. Or frustrated. Or dreaming of doing something different. Whatever the reason, disengagement is a real problem that almost always lowers performance.

A disengaged employee probably isn't interested in feedback about their performance. So instead of hitting them with "constructive criticism," spend some time figuring out the root causes of their disengagement.

Many times, engagement has dropped due to a single aspect of the job—a repetitive task, a specific person or thing in the environment, or something particularly frustrating. Look for these low-hanging problems, then figure out how you can help.

Raising engagement is a critical part of your job that requires many different tools. Some of those tools won't be discussed until much later in the book. In the meantime, here's a reference chart you can refer back to if your employee is disengaged.

Tools	How to Use	When to Use
The engagement activity	Use the engagement activity (see Part 4) to track engagement over time. Use the tools of psychological safety (see Chapter 13) to make it safer for employees to discuss engagement.	Use this when you suspect something isn't right, when something has changed, and periodically, even when things seem fine.
Discover root causes and alternate interests	Figure out the root causes of low engagement. Ask targeted, open-ended questions. Listen carefully, *without judgment*. Learn which parts of the work they prefer to do.	Use this once you know (or suspect) an employee is disengaged.
Remove blockers; adjust the work	Ask yourself what changes can be made. Remove blockers, minimize burdensome tasks, and identify little changes with big impact.	Use this once you've discovered the root cause or alternate interests.
Create opportunities for personal growth	Strong performers crave challenges that help them to become even stronger. Encouraging them to grow professionally (even in small ways) is a fantastic way to increase engagement.	Use this when you have a strong performer who needs new challenges, has been doing the same work for a long time, or is losing interest.

Most companies are open to making changes if it helps an employee perform better. As a people manager, you have the influence to initiate these changes. Use it! Find ways to adjust the work, shuffle teams or projects, or mitigate problems that occur outside of work.

> When COVID-19 emerged, some of my employees found that working from home was extremely distracting. They reported frustration, low engagement, and a decrease in performance. By listening to their needs, we came up with some creative solutions (for example, adjusting work hours, renting temporary office spaces, and providing special equipment). As a people manager, I used my influence to help my employees get back on track, become more engaged, and raise their performance.

Unfortunately, you won't always be able to increase engagement. Worse still, you might discover that engagement wasn't the root cause of a performance problem. In that case, you might have drifted into the fourth feedback scenario.

4. YOUR EMPLOYEE IS (OR IS BECOMING) A LOW PERFORMER

The fourth feedback scenario will require an entirely different set of feedback tools to achieve very different results. Giving feedback to a low performer is a complex subject that we will discuss in depth in the last section of this book.

Before you flag an employee as a low performer, make sure you've already addressed the possibility of confusion, a lack of knowledge/skill, and employee engagement. If you are absolutely certain your employee is a low performer, then you may want to skip ahead to Part 5: What about Low Performers?

5. YOUR EMPLOYEE IS A STRONG PERFORMER

Before we dive into scenario five, let's take a moment to regroup.

To answer the question "How do you give feedback?" I defined feedback as a collection of *tools* used by people managers to achieve *results* related to an employee's performance.

Then I walked through three scenarios: confusion, lack of knowledge/skill, and low engagement. For each, I shared some tools you can use. Then there was the fourth scenario— when you have a low performer, despite your best efforts. We'll tackle that feedback scenario in later chapters.

That leaves us with just one feedback scenario. And, because I've taught many managers, allow me to address the elephant in the room. What I'm about to say is radical. It might sound like it doesn't apply to your company. It might even sound completely wrong.

All I ask is that you consider what I'm about to say with an open mind. I will explain my reasoning in just a moment.

If you aren't dealing with confusion, a lack of knowledge/skill, or low engagement, and the employee is not a low performer, then in all other cases, you are giving feedback to a strong performer.

Let me be completely clear. In the vast majority of cases, you are giving feedback to a strong performer. It's the scenario you face every day with almost all of your employees. Or at least, it should be.

I say "should be" because many managers don't pay enough attention to their strong performers. They assume, "If it ain't broke, don't fix it." Even worse, many managers don't know how to give feedback to their strong performers.

★ ★ ★

Great managers know that most employees are strong performers. They also know that strong performers need to be given the right kind of feedback frequently to excel.

Becoming a great manager requires a paradigm shift in how you think about your employees. And I don't expect you to take this on faith.

In the next chapter, I will walk you through my reasoning. I will explain what it means to be a strong performer. Then I will share some powerful tools that can help your strong performers become even stronger.

Chapter 9

Employee Ratings 2.0

In the vast majority of cases, you are giving feedback to a strong performer. To make sense of this radical statement, consider a hypothetical company, Acme Widgets.

ACME WIDGETS

As a mid-sized company with about one thousand employees, Acme Widgets had a great year. Their CEO invited everyone together for an end-of-year party to celebrate. She praised the staff for their hard work, thanked them for their dedication, and shared the exciting news that the company had grown by a massive 20 percent!

Amidst all the cheering sat Joe, an engineer. Joe wasn't clapping. In fact, he was upset. He had worked really hard during his first year at Acme. He was trying to understand why all of his dedication, collaboration, and hard work had resulted in a yearly rating of "meets expectations."

Instead of feeling excited, Joe started the next year feeling a bit demotivated and a bit less engaged. Joe tried not to let that affect his job performance. Even he would have admitted that he wasn't quite as enthusiastic as he had been his first year.

Joe's situation by itself might not have been a big deal. Unfortunately, Joe was just one of 700 employees who also got a rating of "meets expectations." Many of them were affected in the same way. And those little decreases in enthusiasm compounded as each of those employees brought a bit less energy to each of their teams.

The result was a massive decrease in Acme's potential. Worst of all, no one even recognized this was a problem. To understand why, let's explore three questions:

1. How was Joe *hired*?
2. How was Joe *measured*?
3. How was Joe *rated*?

1. HOW WAS JOE HIRED?

When Joe first saw Acme's job posting, he was excited. He'd been thinking about working at Acme for a long time. So, Joe submitted his application. Lots of other engineers did the same thing. Acme, after all, had a great reputation.

Like many of his competitors, Joe had passion, skill, and aptitude, plus a four-year degree from a major university. Despite the competition, Joe's resume stood out from the rest. He received a callback, spent weeks engaged in interviews, and got the job!

Joe was welcomed onto the team and given everything he needed to succeed. Soon, Joe was contributing real value to his team.

2. HOW WAS JOE MEASURED?

Joe was off to a great start. Now, let's shift our attention to Joe's manager and to Acme's Human Resources (HR) department. They both had a problem.

There is no perfect, objective way to measure Joe's performance. His job is too dynamic. It involves talking with customers, collaborating with team members, and solving complex problems with advanced technologies.

This problem is not unique to Acme Widgets.

It is not possible to precisely measure any employee's performance unless the work is trivial in nature. This is especially true for work done on a team.

This axiom applies to any job requiring advanced knowledge, creative problem-solving, or specialized skills. It also applies to any work involving direct interaction with customers or collaborative work done as part of a larger team.

Lacking a precise, objective way to measure Joe's performance, Acme did what most companies do—they compared Joe's performance to his peers. This method is both relative and subjective.

During the hiring process, Joe was considered the best of

the best. Then Acme's training made him even stronger. The same was true for every other employee at Acme.

Comparing the best-of-the-best employees against each other makes most of them seem about the same. It creates a **bell curve—a graph with the majority of employees near the center, tapering off on each side, forming the shape of a bell**.

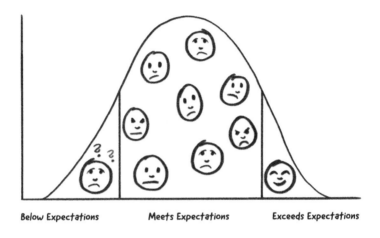

Below Expectations   Meets Expectations   Exceeds Expectations

From Acme's perspective, Joe was right in the middle of an elite, high-performing pack.

Now that we know how Joe is being measured, let's move on to his end-of-year rating.

3. HOW WAS JOE RATED?

Like many companies, Acme used a simple employee rating system with three ranks:

- Exceeds expectations
- Meets expectations
- Below expectations

Every December, Acme managers assigned one of these ranks to each employee. Then they used those ranks to calculate raises, award bonuses, and decide on promotions.

In Joe's case, he was squarely in the middle of the bell curve, so he earned a rating of "meets expectations."

WHY JOE FEELS BAD

The phrase "meets expectations" is a euphemism for "average." Any employee worth keeping is smart enough to realize that.

Unfortunately, "average" is not a form of praise. No one likes to think of themselves as average. Study after study shows that. For example, most adults think they are above-average drivers; most professors believe they are above-average educators; and most people think they have above-average IQs.

In most cases, being called "average" is insulting. Likewise, Joe doesn't want to be told that the two thousand hours he spent helping his team last year was just "average" work. Joe felt insulted, sad, and unappreciated.

IT GETS WORSE

This problem compounds over Joe's entire career.

As we saw earlier, best-of-the-best Joe landed solidly in the middle of an elite, high-performing pack. If he is able to overcome his irritation with being told he is average, he will continue to get better and better at his job. Eventually, he could earn a rating of "exceeds expectations." Finally, Joe would be back to feeling best of the best!

Soon thereafter, Joe would be promoted. Once again, Joe would be back in the middle of the pack, where he would earn a rating of "meets expectations" for several more years. If we imagine Joe's career stretching into the future, we'd see this pattern repeat again and again.

This happens with all Acme employees, in all departments. And again, Acme is not alone. This same pattern repeats in almost every company.

Most companies end up with a bell curve distribution for their end-of-year ratings. That's to be expected. The problem isn't with the bell curve, it's with telling your employees that they are average.

Rating systems based on "meets expectations" cause most employees to feel unappreciated for most of their careers. This is true even when the company itself is doing extremely well.

No one at Acme intended to make Joe feel bad. They certainly didn't intend for hundreds of employees to feel bad. In fact, no company wants their "meets-expectations" employees to feel bad about this. It just happens because companies use an outdated system that's been passed from one company to the next, from one manager to the next, without change.

There is a better way.

THE ALTERNATIVE

Employee Ratings 2.0 is an employee rating system in which reaching the center point of the bell curve is an accomplishment worthy of praise:

- **Star performer**—adds exceptional value, is a leader among their peers, and frequently exceeds the requirements for their title.
- **Strong performer**—consistently adds value, helps the team succeed, and meets the requirements for their title.
- **Low performer**—adds little value, harms the overall team, or fails to meet the minimum requirements for their title.

The key difference with Employee Ratings 2.0 is that it replaces "meets expectations" with "strong performer." And while this might seem like a sleight of hand, in practice, it soon becomes apparent how powerful this change really is.

Earning a rating of strong performer requires engagement, proactive collaboration, and meaningful accomplishment. You can't be a strong performer if you are "quiet quitting," "coasting," or simply "meeting expectations." You have to work hard to rise to the challenges of the day. You have to push yourself to add value, benefit the team, and contribute.

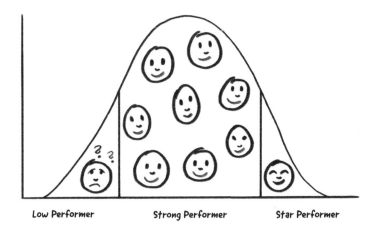

Low Performer   Strong Performer   Star Performer

A cynical person might argue that all I've done is substitute one phrase for another. While there may be some truth to that, it's also true that the language we use shapes the way we think. For example, thinking of my wife as "the love of my life" is dramatically different from labeling her my "ball and chain." The former builds a stronger marriage; the latter tears it down, especially over the long term.

"Meets expectations" is an *insult*. "Strong performer" is a *compliment*. It means you're doing good things for your team, customers, and company. It means your company appreciates you.

Joe wants to be recognized for the value he adds. "Strong performer" accomplishes that perfectly.

In recent years, strong employees have become more valuable than ever. To find, attract, and keep strong performers, smart companies have begun reimagining rating systems like the one used by Acme. For example, Google recently changed its rating system to focus on impact instead of expectations. Instead of using the words "meets" and "exceeds," they use modifiers like "significant," "outstanding," and "transformational."

★ ★ ★

A rating system that includes "meets expectations" is harmful to your employees, company, and customers. Replace it with Employee Ratings 2.0—a system that recognizes that most of your employees are actually strong performers.

Of course, unless you are the head of HR, you probably can't change your company's rating system. Fortunately, that isn't the point.

Thinking of your middle-of-the-bell-curve employees as strong performers is a paradigm shift that will positively impact almost everything you do as a people manager. It will reframe how you think about your employees, give them feedback, and manage their professional development. It will also require new tools for giving feedback. Specifically, tools that help your Strong Performers become *even stronger*.

Chapter 10

Praise Behaviors

Once you begin thinking about your employees as strong performers, you're ready to learn the most powerful way to give them feedback.

Praise the behaviors you want repeated as often as you can.

Figure out which behaviors you want out of your strong performers. Then praise those behaviors whenever you notice them. The more you praise those behaviors, the more your employees will repeat them. It's that simple.

This tool works in both private and public settings. It works with all levels of skill. And it is easy to do. Plus, it feels good for both you and the recipient.

If this makes sense to you, and you are ready to put that into practice, then feel free to skip ahead to the next chapter, where I'll introduce additional feedback tools you can use with your strong performers. If, on the other hand, you need some convincing, or if you just want to know why this works, then read on.

For the rest of this chapter, I'm going to geek out by putting together a little puzzle I call the praise behaviors puzzle. The pieces of this puzzle come from research in the fields of learning, psychology, and motivation. This is the fascinating science that I bypassed at the beginning of Chapter 8.

There are six pieces in the praise behaviors puzzle:

1. Laws of learning
2. Five-to-one rule
3. Fixed mindset
4. Growth mindset
5. Focus on behaviors
6. Incentive theory of motivation

As I introduce each piece, it will become more and more apparent why praising behaviors is so incredibly effective.

GETTING STARTED

To get started, let me share a conversation from one of my one-on-ones.

> I asked Rita, "When was the last time I gave you constructive criticism—you know, corrected your performance or said something negative?"
>
> Rita paused, opened her mouth to say something, and then paused again. "I suppose there was that time you pushed me to decide more quickly. That was...three years ago."

Think about that. It had been three years since I'd given Rita any negative feedback! And throughout those three years, I'd helped her overcome real problems, deal with interpersonal conflicts, and improve both her and her team's performance.

I'd helped her become stronger, and I'd done it relying solely on *positive*, constructive techniques. No criticism was needed; no negative feedback was required.

This is what you're trying to achieve. And there is science to support it.

1. LAWS OF LEARNING

Way back in 1915, a man named Edward Thorndike penned the laws of learning—basic principles that influence our ability to learn. One hundred years later, the laws of learning are still considered core principles of effective education throughout the world.

There are two laws of learning that I want to focus on. Together, they comprise the first piece of the praise behaviors puzzle.

First, the **law of intensity states that intense experiences increase learning outcomes**. The classic example is the child who touches something hot. Getting burned is an intense experience. The brain builds a strong memory to ensure the child learns an essential lesson.

Interestingly, the law of intensity applies to both *negative* and *positive* experiences. From our employee's perspective, both positive and negative feedback can feel intense. Unfortunately, intense negative experiences (such as "constructive criticism") often result in negative learning outcomes—unintentionally learning the wrong things.

Second, the **law of effect states that people learn more while experiencing positive emotions**. A powerful example of this occurs while a child is learning to communicate. Laughing, giggling, and smiling are positive emotions that push the child to continue learning.

Interestingly, some researchers have taken the law of effect even further. They argue that the primary purpose of "fun" itself is to help us learn. The brain releases feel-good hormones to reward us for learning, applying, or mastering new patterns. If that interests you, check out Raph Koster's book *A Theory of Fun for Game Design*.

The takeaway is simple: positive experiences increase how much your employees learn.

Science	Relevance to People Management
Law of intensity	Giving negative feedback to your employee does create intense learning. Unfortunately, you don't know *what* the employee is learning. Often, they learn things you didn't intend, like being afraid to speak up, avoiding collaboration, or defending poor performance. They might learn that they should game the system, that looking good is more important than providing actual value, or that their boss is scary. These things waste energy, reduce collaboration, and keep important information hidden.

Positive feedback is also intense, and it comes with much less baggage. |
| Law of effect (i.e., positive emotions) | Employees learn more when engaged in positive experiences. This applies to routine work, interactions with a manager, and of course, praise. |

When you consider the laws of intensity and effect together, you can begin to see why it's important to praise the behaviors you want repeated. Praise is both intense and positive.

2. FIVE TO ONE

The second piece of our puzzle is the **five-to-one rule—negative interactions are five times as intense as positive interactions.**

Said another way, it takes *five positive* interactions to neutralize *one negative* interaction with your employee. It's sort of like those old-fashioned balance scales. You know, the kind made of shiny brass, with little trays on the left and right, like the scales of justice.

Unfortunately, this scale is rigged. To balance it, you need five times as many positive interactions as negative ones.

In addition, not all interactions are equal. Some weigh more than others. For example, celebrating a major success is more intense than chatting about the weather, even though both are positive.

Five to one is the minimum ratio for maintaining a trusting, successful relationship. If you want a truly strong relationship, the ratio is closer to twenty to one.

Science	Relevance to People Management
Five-to-one rule	Using critical feedback to correct job performance damages your relationship with your employee. Fixing that can require dozens of positives just to get back to a neutral state.
	Use positive interactions, including praise. For an even stronger relationship, use a ratio of twenty positives to one negative. Best of all, drop the one negative altogether.

Five to one is just the starting point. Drs. John and Julie Gottman have been studying relationships for four decades. From their research, they could predict divorce rates by simply counting the number of positive versus negative interactions during a tense moment, such as when a couple is arguing. If that "magic ratio" was less than five to one, the couple was probably headed for a divorce. If on the other hand, it exceeded twenty to one, then they were on the path to an amazing relationship.

When you connect the laws of learning (intensity and positive effect) with the five-to-one rule, the praising behaviors puzzle starts to come together. Praising behaviors is both positive and intense, and it tilts the scale in the correct direction.

To introduce the next pieces of the puzzle, I'm going to share a long, personal story.

A CONTEST

My daughter, Kayla, was absolutely beaming when she got home from school. From her wheelchair, she gave me one of her signature sideways grins.

> "Daddy! I took first place in the writing contest. I won fifty dollars!"

Kayla was a Make-A-Wish child. Her life was filled with incredible challenges, and she was deeply aware of her own fragility. She saw things differently. She wrote from her heart:

"...People shouldn't have to make a law so that others will treat the physically disabled people the way they should be treated. They should do it because they care."

Kayla's essay was awarded first place across the entire school! I lifted her up, hugged her, and spun her around in celebration. We invited the grandparents over to share in our joy. Everyone showered Kayla with praise:

> "You're a natural!"

> "Kayla, you're amazing!"

> "You're so gifted."

Looking back on it now, *the way we praised* Kayla turned out to be one of the biggest regrets of my entire life. At the time, we all thought we were saying the right things. We encouraged Kayla to continue writing.

"Maybe you could join a writing club."

"Or write something for the school newspaper."

"Or start a blog about your life."

To our surprise, Kayla furrowed her brow and looked away.

She didn't join a writing club. Or write for the school newspaper. Or blog about herself. She didn't even enter the same school competition when it came around the next year. In fact, Kayla never wrote anything like that ever again.

YEARS LATER

Years later, I stumbled across *Mindset*, a book by Carol Dweck. Dweck studied how mindset impacts performance. In one study, she gave different instructions to two groups of children—something along these lines:

- To group 1: "You're a natural. This will be easy for you. Please solve these puzzles."
- To group 2: "These puzzles are hard. It's okay to struggle. See what you can learn."

Both sets of instructions seem like the kind of thing that any parent, teacher, or test giver might say. That's what makes the results so astounding. The second group of children were able to solve twice as many puzzles as the first group. *Twice as many!*

> Dweck's research also applies to adults, including me. I spent most of my life with a fixed mindset. When I read Dweck's book, it was like reading my life story. Pages of examples of fixed-mindset language at work, in relationships, and in marriage. It took me years to unlearn. And even to this day, I sometimes have to remind myself that my mistakes don't make me a failure. They are simply opportunities to become *even stronger*.

3. FIXED MINDSET

Dweck's research showed that people (both adults and children) tend to approach a situation in one of two ways. The first is with the fixed mindset, the belief that "I am who I am, and I can't change."

The fixed mindset maintains that a person's skills, capabilities, and future potential are limited by factors outside of themselves.

A person in the fixed mindset believes that their maximum capability is limited by external factors like nature (i.e., genes), nurture (i.e., upbringing), society, money, who you know, or where you went to school. When in the fixed mindset, people learn less, have a lower skill cap, and apply less creative approaches to problems.

It turns out that certain phrases promote a fixed mindset in people, particularly labels such as smart, gifted, or talented. That's what happened in group 1. Dweck used *fixed*-mindset language: "You're a natural. This will be easy for you." When the puzzles were not easy, the children tried fewer creative solutions, learned less, and solved half as many puzzles.

Science	Relevance to People Management
The fixed mindset	Bad things happen when you reinforce fixed mindset tendencies with your employees: • They learn less and hesitate to take risks outside of their comfort zone. • They resist change, adapt slower, and defend processes that don't work. • They waste energy defending poor performance instead of solving problems, collaborating, and getting stronger. • They perform worse, especially in the long term. Avoid any language that promotes a fixed mindset in your employees, such as labeling immutable characteristics.

Just by changing the words you use, you can decrease how often your employees adopt a fixed mindset. That alone will increase your employees' performance, which is why it's the third piece of our praise behaviors puzzle.

There are many famous examples of the fixed mindset in sports. Consider the "prodigy" who shouts, curses, and smashes things after a loss. While it's normal to have negative feelings after a setback, these emotional outbursts can be evidence that the "prodigy" is struggling with the fixed mindset.

4. GROWTH MINDSET

The next piece to our praise behaviors puzzle is the growth mindset. **The growth mindset maintains that our skills, capabilities, and future potential have no limit.** It asserts that we can always become better than we are right now, including mastering things that once seemed impossible.

The growth mindset is summed up by the slogan, "Failure is part of the path that leads to victory." It is the basic assumption that underpins the title of my leadership workshop, "Lead; Refine; Repeat."

The growth mindset is why I think of leadership as a journey, rather than a destination.

Fortunately, just as with the fixed mindset, certain phrases promote a growth mindset in other people. That includes phrases such as trying, embracing failure, or anything that focuses on learning. That's what happened with the second group of children. Dweck used *growth* mindset language: "It's okay to struggle. See what you can learn." This reduced the children's anxiety about performing, increased creative thinking, and led to twice the performance.

Science	Relevance to People Management
The growth mindset	Good things happen when you reinforce growth mindset tendencies with your employees: • They learn faster, develop a broader range of skills, and solve problems more creatively. • They adapt better to change, embrace new processes sooner, and have increased resilience after setbacks. • They collaborate more effectively, help their teams improve, and work harder to become stronger. • They perform better in almost every conceivable way, especially in the long run. Focus on behaviors that lead to learning, growth, and improvement. Emphasize progress rather than outcomes.

Promoting a growth mindset will increase your employee's performance over time. It's the fourth piece of our praise behaviors puzzle.

5. FOCUS ON BEHAVIORS

The next piece of the praise behaviors puzzle may be the most important of all. The core problem with fixed-mindset language is that it labels the immutable characteristics of a person.

Think back to the story of my daughter, Kayla. We used labels like "good," "worthy," "gifted," "skilled," "amazing," "talented," and "natural." Those words put her on a pedestal, proclaiming her the victor, indelibly judging her as a person. Those labels reinforced her own tendency toward a fixed mindset.

Right away, Kayla began to question whether she was worthy of all that praise. What if her next effort fell short? Instead of trying again and risking being labeled a "failure," she took the easier route, which meant not writing, ever again.

The lesson is clear. Labels are a form of judgment that promotes the fixed mindset. That's true when the labels are attached to the person. It's also true when the labels are connected to the outcomes/results of their effort. It's even true when the labels are positive, as in the compliment, "You're a natural."

Don't use labels. Instead, focus on behaviors. Talk about what your employee *has done*, *is doing*, or *will do*. These are behaviors, and behaviors can be changed.

If you aren't sure how to do this, try focusing on the effort. For example, "You worked hard" or "You took proactive steps." Alternatively, emphasize how much they've grown instead of what they've accomplished.

Science	Relevance to People Management
Focus on behaviors	Avoid language that labels the person. Instead, focus on the behaviors because behaviors can be changed. Also, minimize language that labels the outcome/results. If you decide to praise the results, try to connect it with the behaviors that led to those results.
	Avoid judgmental praise like "You were great in today's meeting." Instead, focus on the behaviors, "You prepared thoroughly, had all the research you needed, and kept your cool, even when asked tough questions."

With Kayla, we could have praised how hard she'd worked, how many times she'd iterated her paper, or how vulnerable she'd been by sharing her personal stories with everyone at school. That behavior-focused language would have encouraged a growth mindset, which could have made her less afraid of trying again. Of course, I didn't know any of that at the time.

> Praising an employee's immutable characteristics can make them feel uncomfortable. I have come to realize that when an employee says, "I don't like to be praised," what they actually mean is, "I don't like to be judged, especially for things I cannot change." Praising their behaviors rarely makes people feel judged.

6. INCENTIVE THEORY OF MOTIVATION

The final piece of the praise behaviors puzzle comes from the **incentive theory of motivation, which states that**

humans are motivated *toward* rewards, especially praise from others.

That's a pretty basic concept. It doesn't seem all that insightful until you combine it with everything else you've just learned.

When you praise *behaviors*, you are praising something your employee *did* before, not something they are doing right now or in the future. In a sense, the positive feedback only applies to the past. It's sort of old news. It already happened.

To continue being worthy of the praise you've already given— one of the most motivating rewards there is—your employee must continue performing that same behavior in the future!

Science	Relevance to People Management
Incentive theory of motivation	Employees are highly motivated by the positive affirmation of others. Because behaviors are something the employee did in the past, when you praise the behaviors that led to success, the employee will be motivated to repeat them in the future to remain worthy of the praise.

This final piece brings all of the science together to create a single, cohesive image.

Technically, the incentive theory of motivation also includes the idea that we are motivated to avoid punishment. It's the idea of the "carrot and the stick." The carrot (positive) pulls us toward something and the stick (negative) pushes us away from something. Both are motivating, and both have potential problems.

The problem with the stick is that it often has negative side effects, such as decreasing learning, reducing collaboration, and creating myopic views of how we solve problems. The problem with the carrot is that it can promote a fixed mindset if you are using labels such as "You're a natural." Praising behaviors is a carrot without either of those problems.

PUTTING THE PUZZLE TOGETHER

Once again, here are the six pieces of our praise behaviors puzzle:

1. Laws of learning
2. Five-to-one rule
3. Fixed mindset
4. Growth mindset
5. Focus on behaviors
6. Incentive theory of motivation

This is the science behind why praise works so well. The picture is now complete.

Praise the behaviors you want repeated as often as you can. This promotes learning, creative thinking, and high performance. It also motivates your employees to repeat behaviors that are critical to their team's success.

It took me a while to get the hang of this new tool. It will take you time too. To help you along, I've included several examples. Those in the first half of the table praise behaviors when the individual/team is *succeeding*. The examples in the second half of the table praise behaviors even though the individual/team is *struggling*.

Individual Success	Example of Praising the Behaviors They Did Well
Employee completed an investigation on time.	"Thank you for jumping on this right away. I appreciate the thoroughness of your investigation, and how quickly you turned this around."
Employee iterated without attachment (see Chapter 11).	"I love that you brought *three* different ideas to the meeting and were able to highlight the strengths and weaknesses of each."
Employee pivoted quickly.	"Thank you for addressing your team's concerns and helping everyone to adapt to the added requirements and earlier deadline. Your leadership was pivotal!"
Team Success	**Example of Praising the Behaviors They Did Well**
Team pivoted to meet a new deadline.	"Thank you, everyone, for pausing your prior commitments. You asked questions, worked collaboratively, and attacked the new deadline with laser focus."

Individual Is Struggling	Example of Praising the Behaviors They Are Still Learning
Employee is working through a conflict.	"Thank you for taking this situation seriously. I imagine it's been hard to learn a new communication tool, set aside some of your internal stories, and be vulnerable as you try to improve your working relationship with Joe."
Employee stayed focused, despite a lack of interest.	"I know this wasn't your favorite task. Thank you for keeping the intensity up so we could hit the deadline. Because of your dedication, this will soon be behind us."
Employee is improving in a weak area.	"I appreciate how hard you've worked to overcome this challenge. It's clear you've been asking for guidance, taking in feedback, and communicating your progress. All of this is making you stronger."
Team Is Struggling	Focus on the Behaviors That Will Lead to Future Success
A project failed (e.g., over budget, behind schedule, or poorly received).	"It's been a challenging month with several setbacks. And while it's important to acknowledge the difficulties, it's also true that in the final two weeks, we came together, prioritized appropriately, and collaborated without conflict. It's the best teamwork we've ever had—and it's how we're going to succeed next time."

Take a closer look at that last example. Note that I did not criticize the team for past mistakes. The long-term cost of broad-brushed, intense, negative feedback to the entire team would have been catastrophically damaging. And it would not have changed the result or helped the team grow to meet their next challenge.

Never criticize an entire team publicly. If you must criticize, do it privately, either one on one or in small groups.

Is praising behaviors just a form of manipulation? This is a serious question that good managers often ask. The definition of "manipulation" includes ideas like "deviously," "deceptive behavior," or "for personal gain." If you are using praise for any of those reasons, then yes, you are manipulating your employees. That will destroy trust. If, instead, you are using your influence to increase engagement, clarify expectations, and help your employees thrive, then you aren't manipulating them; you're becoming a great manager!

YOUR TURN

Here are three feedback scenarios you can practice. For each scenario, imagine you are actually talking to the other person. Find a quiet place where you can *say the words out loud*—that will help you to learn faster (i.e., the law of intensity).

1. Easy scenario—praising behaviors in relationships. You are standing in the living room with your boyfriend/girlfriend/husband/wife/lover/partner. You want to tell them, "You are gorgeous." Instead, find an authentic way to praise their behaviors.

2. Medium scenario—praising a peer's success. You are talking with a peer at work. You were impressed with something they did. Now, praise them to their face, focusing only on their behaviors. For bonus points, praise their growth.

3. Hard scenario—be vulnerable. You are having a one-on-one with an employee who struggled through weeks of setbacks before finally scoring a major victory for the team. For this scenario, share a story about overcoming your own struggles. Talk about the challenges you faced, how you resolved them, and what you learned from the experience. Focus on your behaviors. Then relate this back to your employee by praising their behaviors.

As you practice these scenarios, think about what it means to praise the behavior instead of labeling the person. It will feel awkward at first. You will hesitate, use clumsy phrases, and get stuck. And as we know from the growth mindset, if you keep trying, you will eventually master this technique.

The brain is an amazing pattern-matching machine. It looks for patterns in everything from the weather to the expressions on other people's faces. In his book *The Power of Habit,* Charles Duhigg explains how the brain uses those patterns to form habits.

A habit involves a *cue*, a *behavior*, and a *reward*. The *cue* can be anything—a sound, smell, feeling, touch, gesture, word, phrase, or facial expression. Similarly, the *behavior* can be almost anything too—something you say, do, or even think. The *reward* is where things get interesting.

Imagine stepping off the curb into the road. You will instinctively look left and right before you proceed. You don't even think about it. It's a habit. In fact, it's such a compelling habit that most people can't imagine stepping off the curb without looking both ways first. If you tried it in real life, your brain would fight you, increasing your anxiety until you complied.

This helps us understand how habits work. The cue is approaching the curb; the behavior is looking left and right; and the reward is putting a stop to that nagging feeling that you haven't done what you're supposed to do.

This cue-behavior-reward cycle is critical to survival. You literally couldn't make it through a single day without the thousands of habits that make it possible to drink from a cup, tie your shoes, or walk without falling down. Habits are a fundamental part of being human, which means you can leverage them to become an even more effective people manager. Praise the behaviors you want repeated to help your employees form habits that make them even more successful.

★ ★ ★

In this chapter, I shared the single most powerful tool for providing feedback to your strong performers: praise the behaviors you want repeated.

Of course, the tool assumes that you know which behaviors you want repeated. So study your employees, figure out which behaviors lead to success, and then begin praising them, as often as you can.

The more you do this, the sooner your employees will internalize the drive to repeat those behaviors until they eventually become habits. At that point, you can focus on new behaviors that will help them become even stronger.

This cycle is part of what makes praise so incredibly effective. It works with Star Performer Sally, Strong Performer Joe, and everyone in between.

While praising behaviors is by far your most effective feedback tool, it does require time to take effect. And sometimes, you need to provide more immediate guidance.

Chapter 11

When Time Is Short

Praise is powerful. It helps your employee build more effective habits, and habits take time to build. Here are five tools for giving feedback to strong performers when time is short:

1. Even stronger
2. Ask permission
3. Iterate without attachment
4. Self-evaluation
5. One thing at a time

1. EVEN STRONGER

Can you make your feedback sound less critical? Yes, by adding just two words, "even stronger."

This technique is super simple and surprisingly powerful. Whenever you're sharing feedback with a strong performer, think in terms of helping them to become "even stronger." It implies that their work is already strong (which it is).

For example:

- "Today's practice session was much stronger. You shared powerful stories, started with "why," and replaced the walls of text with short bullet points and captivating images. If you continue practicing your conclusion, it will be even stronger at tomorrow's event."
- "Your report hit the high points, had plenty of details, and stuck to the point. It's really strong as is. If you are looking for ways to make it even stronger, consider adding a short synopsis and re-stating your takeaways on your last slide."

We'll discuss this technique in more detail in Part 4: What Aren't Your Employees Telling You? In the meantime, give it a try. Pay attention to how it changes how you give feedback and how your employees feel about receiving it.

2. ASK PERMISSION

If your strong performer needs a *lot* of additional guidance, consider asking for permission before giving them feedback. It's surprisingly effective.

Consider the time that I asked Rita to write a cross-team report. It was an unusual request, well outside of her comfort zone.

> "Thank you for looking into this. I appreciate your thoughtful, quick exploration of the problem. Your careful attention to the details helps to highlight the nuances that could easily be overlooked." Then, I paused for a moment before asking, "*Would you like some feedback that could make the report even stronger?*"

In the above example, I combined three techniques: praise behaviors, even stronger, and ask permission. I started off by highlighting concrete behaviors to reinforce that Rita is a strong performer and to make the conversation feel safer.

Then I asked Rita for permission while also including the words, "even stronger." This empowered Rita, while also making it clear that I was about to offer expert advice—something most strong performers crave.

The pause in the middle inserted a distinct break between my discussion of what she'd done well and my introducing what might be improved. This separation reinforced that her original work was strong and preserves the positivity of the interaction, ultimately increasing learning.

Employees will usually say "yes" when you ask permission to give them feedback. Sometimes they will say "no." If you're going to ask, be mindful that your employee might not be ready to hear your feedback at that moment. If you are planning to give feedback whether or not they want to hear it, don't ask permission. Otherwise, you'll destroy trust.

> Another one of the laws of learning is the law of readiness—people learn more when they are motivated to learn. When we ask our employees whether or not they'd like feedback, we are empowering them to decide when they are ready to grow. This increases their motivation, which increases learning outcomes.

3. ITERATE WITHOUT ATTACHMENT

Whether it's a simple piece of art, a press release, or an entire book, no product is ever perfect the first time around. Excellence requires revision, iteration, and refinement. That's why high-performing teams have multiple stages of review.

If you know your employee's work will require multiple iterations, then make it clear in advance that you plan to iterate on their work.

In addition, take steps to minimize their emotional attachment to the work. When employees become emotionally attached, they iterate slower, resist feedback, and fail to recognize the flaws in an idea. They also become more myopic, which limits the range of possible solutions they will consider for hard problems.

In Rita's case, I asked her to send her first draft directly to me, instead of sending it to the entire studio. She expected me to iterate it. She understood that iteration was a fundamental part of producing great work.

Making the changes myself was a faster way to give feedback to Rita. She studied what I did to make the report stronger. It helped her improve without feeling judged, criticized, or rejected.

If you intend to use this tool often, consider adding "iterated without attachment" to the list of behaviors that you praise. Make sure everyone understands that the work belongs to the group, not the individual. Over time, it will become a part of your team culture.

4. SELF-EVALUATION

Strong performers are often able to identify both what needs to be improved and how. These are perfect opportunities to switch to the coaching leadership style.

A mentor once told me that coaching means asking the right questions. With the right questions, you can guide your employees to discover truths for themselves. Here are a few examples of what I mean:

- How do you think it went?
- What struggles did you face?
- What would you like to do even better?
- What did you learn that you can apply next time?
- What else?

When you are coaching, try not to provide all the answers. The search for the answers is an important part of the learning experience. It encourages your employee to take ownership of their own performance, which boosts their long-term engagement.

For example, let's assume that we hadn't planned on iterating Rita's report, and instead, she shared her original version with the entire studio. In that case, in our next one-on-one, I would have facilitated Rita's self-evaluation.

"Thank you for taking the lead, Rita. You took the time to gather information from the other departments, and still got it out super fast. Now that you've had time to reflect, how do you feel about your work on the report?"

From there, I would shift to coaching mode by asking thoughtful, probing questions that would encourage self-reflection. I would listen patiently, be present, and find out what additional feedback she needed from me.

Self-reflection is just as valuable when everything goes well. You can use it to call attention to already exemplary work or invite your employee to explore how they could become even stronger.

I need to add a note of caution about the self-reflection tool. Some employees can be quite critical of their own performance, particularly if they hold themselves to incredibly high standards. Try not to minimize their concerns; the intensity they feel creates opportunities for massive growth.

Your job as a people manager is to use your influence to help your employees thrive over the long term. If your employee has identified areas of growth, be their coach, focus on the future, and help them discover ways to become even stronger.

Of course, don't forget to praise the behaviors that led to strong performance, including the fact that they are self-evaluating their own work.

5. ONE THING AT A TIME

If there are multiple problems that need to be addressed, try to focus on the one thing that's most important. Leave smaller concerns for another time.

Throwing everything at your strong performer can drastically increase the intensity of their experience. While intensity can increase learning, it can also trigger defensiveness, confusion, or other negative learning outcomes, such as feeling overwhelmed.

Instead, address only what's most important. That will maximize their learning.

Feedback is not something you schedule once a year, once a quarter, or once a month. It's something you do day in and day out as opportunities arise. And it absolutely matters *how* you do it. So let's recap what we've learned.

There are only five feedback scenarios:

1. Your employee is *confused.*
2. Your employee *lacks knowledge/skill.*
3. Your employee is *disengaged.*
4. Your employee is (or is becoming) a *low performer.*
5. Your employee is a *strong performer.*

The first three scenarios happen from time to time with all employees. The fourth scenario is covered in detail in Part 5: What about Low Performers? The last scenario is the most common scenario of all—it's where you will do your most important work.

Learn how to praise behaviors, iterate without attachment, use the phrase "even stronger," ask for permission, and self-evaluate. Then weave these techniques into meetings, emails/

texts, and one-on-ones. Watch for behaviors you can praise, then praise them.

Think of your employees as Strong Performers and give feedback that helps them become even stronger. That's how you answer the second question. Now, let's tackle the third one.

Part 3

WHAT AREN'T YOUR EMPLOYEES TELLING YOU?

Chapter 12

Failure to Communicate

So far, we've tackled question 1, "Do your employees know what's expected of them?" and question 2, "How do you give feedback?" You've learned numerous tools, the science that explains why those tools work, and a mindset for seeing your employees as strong performers.

It's a lot of material, so you might be feeling overwhelmed. Fortunately, you don't need to master all of it right now. Start by asking the hard questions, searching for the answers, and working to become a stronger manager today than you were yesterday.

When you're ready, there's another problem you need to solve.

Your employees aren't telling you everything you need to know. Not just a few things—lots of things. And many of those things directly impact their job performance.

What you don't know about, you can't fix.

Fortunately, this is another problem that great managers can solve. To understand how they solve it, let me tell you about the year I spent as a research fellow at a medical school.

OFF TO MEDICAL SCHOOL

To my surprise, I went from writing software every day to watching live surgeries in an actual operating room. It was an intense transition that taught me valuable lessons about communication—most importantly, that sharing information is hard, even among highly trained professionals, and even when lives are on the line.

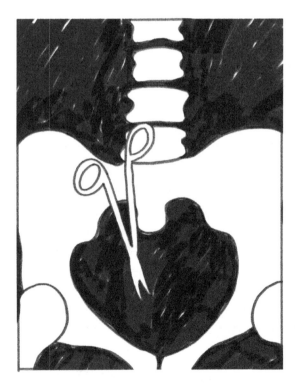

This image is an example of a **sentinel event, a critical medical emergency caused by human error.** Research shows that 70 percent of sentinel events are caused by breakdowns in communication. In other words, someone knew something and didn't share it with other members of the medical team.

Since the right person didn't know about the problem, no one fixed it, and bad things happened.

The 1998 landmark paper, "To Err Is Human," kicked off two decades of research demonstrating that the root cause of most medical errors was a simple breakdown in communication. Those breakdowns contributed to almost one hundred thousand deaths per year in the United States. alone. Future studies proved this was a worldwide phenomenon, which led the World Health Organization (WHO) to classify medical errors as the number one healthcare problem facing the world.

Nowadays, hospitals have implemented "time out" protocols, mandatory communication training, and strict procedures for confirming patient identity. Some hospitals even mandate same-color scrubs to reduce the power differential among staff members. Unfortunately, even with all of these changes, medical errors resulting from poor communication are still one of the leading causes of death today.

WHY AREN'T PEOPLE TALKING?

This baffled me. As a software engineer, I didn't face life-and-death decisions on a daily basis at work. It was hard for me to understand why a healthcare professional would withhold information that could save someone's life.

With further research, I uncovered two clues that helped me understand.

The first clue is that healthcare is hierarchical. Think of this in terms of high status vs. low status. The doctors and surgeons have high status. Conversely, the nurses, assistants, and other professionals have low status.

The second clue is that people with low status become more fearful when working with someone of high status.

This is due to **Maslow's hierarchy of needs, which outlines five tiers of human needs: physiological, safety, belonging, esteem, and self-actualization.** These five tiers must generally be met in order, from bottom to top. For example, if you are literally dying from lack of food/water, then you aren't worried about self-esteem.

Self–
actualizing

Esteem
(mastery, respect)

Belonging
(love, friends, connection)

Safety

Physiological
(food, rest, biological)

With these two clues in mind, take a closer look at the second tier in Maslow's pyramid: safety. The second tier includes the ability to earn a living, put food on the table, and provide for loved ones.

In practical terms, people with high status have substantial influence over the second-tier needs of someone with low-status. That power differential makes low-status employees more fearful.

This is why a surgical assistant might not point out that the surgeon has inadvertently contaminated a sterile field. It's also why a nurse might not question prepping the left knee when the patient had gestured several times at their right knee during intake.

They don't feel safe.

The same is true at your work. There is an imbalance of power between you and your employees. You have influence over hiring/firing, raises, and promotions. You are threatening.

In fact, you are the most threatening thing in most of your employees' lives.

This impacts every conversation you have. It stifles open collaboration. It makes your employees feel unsafe. It causes them to shy away from sensitive topics, disagreements, and hard questions. It prevents you from learning what's most important.

The result? Your employees have conflicts, concerns, and confusion that they aren't sharing. If trained medical professionals are afraid to speak up when lives are on the line, then it's easy to imagine how your own employees might be similarly impacted.

MEET SHERI

To see how this applies outside of healthcare, meet Sheri.

Sheri was a valuable member of my engineering team—a strong performer. She seemed engaged and happy. Then one day, without warning, Sheri submitted her resignation, packed up her family, and moved to another state to take a higher-paying position doing exactly the same thing.

Despite numerous opportunities in one-on-ones, Sheri had never once raised concerns about her salary. Why not? Because it was less scary to upend her entire life than it was to ask for a raise.

People managers have high status; employees have low status. This imbalance of power makes your employees afraid to tell you things that are really important. Like the fact that the idea you suggested last week led to a critical flaw in the design of the product. Or that one of your best employees has started looking for a new job because they are bored.

If you don't know about those things, you can't do anything about them.

It's time to learn how to make it safe and keep the conversation flowing.

Chapter 13

Make It Safe

You have high status; your employees have low status. This power differential causes your employees to avoid raising sensitive topics, such as:

- Boredom
- An inability to focus due to distractions
- Conflicts with other employees
- Loss of faith in the company's mission/leaders
- Awareness that a peer isn't performing
- Lack of growth opportunities
- Imposter syndrome
- A self-rating of low performance
- Salary

Left unaddressed, these concerns lead to confusion, disengagement, and low performance. Of course, you can't address these concerns if you don't know about them.

Worse still, it's not enough to just tell your employees, "You can talk to me about anything." Those words mean nothing unless your employee truly believes that it is safe.

Psychological safety is the belief that you won't be rejected, embarrassed, or punished for sharing ideas, asking questions, or making mistakes.

If you reject an employee's bad idea out of hand, they will be less inclined to speak up later when they notice a critical flaw that could cost millions of dollars!

If you embarrass an employee in front of others, that employee and *everyone else* will feel less safe. Avoid using sarcasm, teasing, and jabs. Ditch the half-jests that some people refer to as "bro-talk." Even if you personally enjoy that sort of banter, don't use it at work.

If you must highlight an employee's mistake, then do so in a one-on-one, where the stakes are much less scary. Even then, take the time to use the techniques in the earlier chapters.

The opposite of a psychologically safe environment is the **culture of silence, in which employees hide their mistakes and those of others to prevent people from getting in trouble.**

Being rejected, embarrassed, or punished makes people feel more afraid in the future. It's why nurses and surgical assistants don't speak up, even though someone might die. It's also why I can say what follows with confidence.

You cannot become a great manager until you learn to make it safe.

Start with the bare minimum—don't reject, embarrass, or punish your employees for sharing ideas, asking questions, or making mistakes. Then begin using these five techniques:

1. Be present.
2. Use active listening.
3. Be vulnerable.
4. Admit fallibility.
5. State it explicitly.

1. BE PRESENT

The simplest way to increase psychological safety is to be fully present in every one-on-one.

When you are present, you convey to your employee that they are heard, valued, and respected. This reinforces the message that what they have to say is important. That, in turn, increases psychological safety.

Being present includes the obvious stuff like not being distracted by text messages, emails, and notifications. It also includes the less obvious stuff like not getting lost in your head or planning what you're going to say next while your employee is talking. Focus on the here and now.

2. USE ACTIVE LISTENING TECHNIQUES

Being fully present is a prerequisite to **active listening, which is a collection of techniques to be a better listener and receiver of information.**

Basic Tools	How to Use
Non-verbal communication	Maintain eye contact, relax your posture, face your employee, nod as appropriate, sit/stand at the same height, and remove physical barriers (such as tables or monitors). Non-verbal communication can be reinforced with simple utterances, such as "uh huh."
Defer judgment	Listen first, judge later (or not at all). Even if some details are not perfectly accurate, don't rush to correct them. This is similar to the approach used in the brainstorming step of the expectations activity.
Pause	Don't be in a hurry to skip to the ending, make your point, or reach a decision. Allow periods of silence. Don't interrupt.

Advanced Tools	How to Use
Ask clarifying questions	Periodically ask for more information. Create additional opportunities for them to share information. Use expressions like "Tell me more," "Can you explain?" and "What else?"
Reflect	Periodically restate what you are hearing from your perspective in your own words. For example, "To reflect back, when such-and-such happened, that made you feel..."
Recap	At the end of the conversation (or at major breakpoints), take time to summarize key points. When decisions are made or actions need to be taken, make sure to restate them clearly.
Check for understanding	Confirm that both parties understand and agree on the key points. This includes reflecting, recapping, and asking clarifying questions. It means checking explicitly instead of assuming.

While these ideas are simple in theory, mastering them will take time. So give them a try, reflect on how it went, and try again next time.

If you find yourself a bit confused about exactly how to use them, consider this general principle: seek first to understand your employees—then, to be understood.

3. BE VULNERABLE

It matters that you listen. It also matters that you are vulnerable.

Admitting vulnerability does *not* mean sharing details about your *personal life*. Instead, it means being transparent about your own fears, concerns, and challenges *related to your work*. That might mean admitting you don't have all the answers, you aren't sure what happens next, or things didn't work out as you'd hoped or expected.

Here are some examples of what being vulnerable sounds like:

Area of Concern	Example
Loss of faith	"We've had a lot of changes in the past six months. My boss left, we got a new studio head, and now the vision has changed. I'm a bit rattled myself. How are you doing?"
Lack of growth opportunities	"The last few months have been kind of repetitive. Fix a bug; ship an update; repeat. I'm pretty sure I could do this with my eyes closed. How are you keeping yourself challenged?"
Inability to focus	"When we started working remotely, I had a lot of trouble focusing. Grocery deliveries, barking dogs, and clanking dishwashers. How's your situation working out now?"

Knowing that you've had a similar concern makes it safe for your employee to express their own concerns.

Caution: Do not be inauthentic. Inventing fake concerns, exaggerating situations, or pretending to be vulnerable is a sure way to undermine trust. That will reduce psychological safety, which defeats the point.

If you want to learn more about the power of vulnerability as a leader, consider reading Brené Brown's book *Dare to Lead*. As she explains it, "Vulnerability involves uncertainty, risk, and emotional exposure." If you just want a summary of her ideas, check out her TED Talk, "The Power of Vulnerability." With tens of millions of views, it's one of the top ten TED Talks.

4. ADMIT FALLIBILITY

The corollary to being vulnerable is admitting your own fallibility.

As a research fellow, I saw firsthand how powerful it was when a surgeon (high-status) admitted their own fallibility. I even learned that admitting fallibility is part of their gold standard for starting any surgical procedure:

> "Listen up. There are plenty of ways we can make mistakes today. I'll make them, and you'll make them too. The real mistake is not speaking up. If anything seems out of the ordinary, anything at all, you must speak up. Now, let's introduce ourselves."

When the highest-status person admits fallibility, they make it less threatening for others to speak up. Remember, it's rarely the mistakes that kill people (for example, a wrong medicine or a drop in blood pressure), it's the fact that no one is talking about the mistakes until it's too late.

If taking ten seconds to admit fallibility can save thousands of lives, imagine what it can do for you as a people manager when lives aren't on the line.

Here are some examples of what it looks like to admit fallibility at work:

Area of Concern	Example
Starting a risky project (i.e., beginning a surgery)	"This is a high-risk project. I will make mistakes, you will too. To succeed, we need to talk openly, and that includes raising concerns, even if they seem small."
Imposter syndrome	"Early in my career, my boss quit. I went from engineer to engineering *manager* overnight. I made so many mistakes. What a mess."
Conflicts with other employees	"Remember Jeff? He and I always seemed to be on opposite sides. It was tense. Finally, we took the time to share our perspectives. Our relationship slowly improved. As cliché as it sounds, we did eventually become friends."

Admitting fallibility was hard for me at first. The more I practiced it, the easier it became. Nowadays, I am much more willing to admit fallibility to my employees. This makes it safer for them to take risks, talk about their mistakes, and share their challenges. That helps me discover what they otherwise wouldn't be saying so I can help them become even stronger.

5. STATE IT EXPLICITLY

If you are already working to cultivate a culture of psychological safety, and you already suspect there's a topic that your employees might be afraid to discuss, then you have an additional option. You can explicitly tell your employees which topics are safe to discuss.

The idea is to move directly toward the concern, make it safe for them to talk about it, and then actively listen. Here are three examples of making sensitive topics safe.

Area of Concern	Team Example
Salary	"Let's talk openly. Unemployment is low, inflation is up, and we've lost some good folks recently. I'm working with HR to raise salaries. In the meantime, if you are concerned about your salary, please come talk to me. I want to hear your thoughts. It's safe."

Area of Concern	Individual Example
Self-rating of low performance	"Earlier, you hinted that you had a concern that you might not be as productive as you'd like to be. I want to hear your thoughts about that. Tell me more."
Boredom	"You've been working on that project almost a year—same project, same team, same work. I suspect it may be getting a bit boring. I want to check in and see how you are doing."

For clarity, this technique only works if you have cultivated psychological safety using the earlier techniques. Remember, talking to you about sensitive topics is scary. Your employees have to trust that they won't be rejected, embarrassed, or punished in any way.

PUTTING IT ALL TOGETHER

I often begin my one-on-ones with a short open-ended question: "What's on your mind?" Of course, asking an open-ended question is just the beginning. Consider my one-on-one conversation with Larry.

After some chit-chat about the weather, I cleared my throat, paused briefly, and adopted a more serious tone. I asked Larry, "What's on your mind for today?"

Larry replied instantly, "Oh nothing much. I'm doing good."

While Larry had plenty to say about the weather, I sensed he was avoiding something important. I said, "This week was rough. I'm sad about losing our tech lead. I keep wondering what I could have done better. And then we had those setbacks earlier in the week. So, in that context, seriously, what's on your mind?"

From there, I stayed present, used active listening, and asked follow-up questions. All of this made it safe for Larry to tell me that he was having trouble staying focused at work. He found the nearby meetings too distracting—and that was impacting his work for about four hours every Monday and Wednesday. That was news to me. And it was something I could address.

Like you, I have high status relative to my employees. This makes it less likely that they will share important concerns with me. To overcome that challenge, I do everything I can to make it safe, starting with the five techniques I just shared.

Good managers work hard to increase psychological safety. Great managers go one step further, actively working to keep the conversation flowing.

Chapter 14

Keep the Conversation Flowing

Ever seen someone kayaking down a swiftly moving river? They dodge, weave, and flow smoothly around obstacles. Even in the wildest currents, the kayak just seems to know where to go. It looks fluid, organic, and almost effortless.

Of course, it's not effortless. The kayaker has planned specific tactics for each twist and turn. They have worked hard to build up their muscles. They are extremely focused on steering the boat while also allowing it to flow naturally with the contours of the river.

As a people manager, that's how conversations with your employees should feel. The kayaker doesn't fight the river, and you don't fight your employees. Instead, you do everything you can to keep the conversation flowing so you can answer the question, "What aren't my employees telling me?"

Here are six techniques to keep the conversation flowing:

1. Use the phrase "Tell me more."
2. Highlight areas of agreement.
3. Be a helpful coach.
4. Ask open-ended questions.
5. Stop asking "why" questions.
6. Stop arguing the details.

The first four are tools you should use more often. The last two highlight habits you should avoid.

1. USE THE PHRASE "TELL ME MORE"

In my experience, employees with significant concerns are often in a strange mental state. They are snared halfway between fear and hope—fear of what might happen and hope that things will get better.

Asking your employee "Tell me more" makes them feel heard, increases psychological safety, and invites them to say whatever else is on their mind.

"Tell me more" is particularly effective when you sense your employee is dancing on the edge of a sensitive concern. "Tell me more" lets them know it's safe to continue without constraint, limitation, or judgment. It keeps the conversation flowing.

There are other phrases that work just as well as "Tell me more." For example, "What else?" and "Go on."

2. HIGHLIGHT AREAS OF AGREEMENT

If you stop to think about it, you and your employees agree on almost everything about the work. This is true even when you are having a heated discussion. It just doesn't always seem like it because you've allowed yourself to get sucked into a vortex of unproductivity over tiny details.

To prevent that from happening, listen for areas of agreement. Then highlight them.

The basic idea is to slow down, listen, and make an intentional effort to call out things you *do* agree on. That could be the prior work, backstory, intentions, effort, teamwork, core vision, root cause, or any number of positive behaviors.

It could even be things that have nothing to do with the discussion topic itself, like the fact that your employee had the courage to raise their concerns, that they are trying to become stronger, or that they're passionate about their work.

Taking time to highlight these areas of agreement will strengthen your relationship, reinforce the behaviors you want repeated, and increase the positive momentum of the conversation.

Amount of Agreement	How to Keep the Conversation Flowing	Example
When you mostly agree with your employee	This is the most common case, so don't ignore it. Take a moment to highlight the things you agree with before moving on.	"I agree, things have been kind of repetitive lately. Thank you for raising your concern. Let's talk about what might help."
When you disagree on a few minor details	Minor disagreements can easily escalate. So, slow down, avoid making broad generalizations, and help the employee master the material. In addition, take a moment to decide what's most important to you: correcting a few minor details or ensuring the vision, expectations, and big picture are correct.	"I really like where you're going with this. It helps us release products sooner, invites the other departments to participate, and sounds robust. I have some thoughts that could make it even stronger."
When you significantly disagree	While rare, this situation can damage both trust and your long-term relationship with your strong performer. Be careful. Take a moment to zoom out to topics that everyone agrees on. Revisit the vision/objectives. Then highlight the strengths of the alternatives so the employee feels heard.	"Let's slow down. We've confirmed the app is crashing, verified the impact on customers, and investigated possible causes. We think we can make a fix, and there are several paths we can take. Let's walk through each of the scenarios again."

Listening for areas of agreement is not the same as avoiding problems, disagreements, or concerns. It is a way of emphasizing that you and your employees agree on lots and lots of things—and you are, in fact, on the same team.

It keeps the conversation flowing, which makes it easier to

navigate through the tough spots. It also takes advantage of the science we learned while putting together the praise behaviors puzzle back in Chapter 10, including the five-to-one rule and the laws of intensity and effect.

Highlighting areas of agreement creates intense, positive interactions that build momentum. That's almost always helpful, regardless of the situation.

Have you ever watched improvisational actors perform in front of a live audience? The best example is the show *Whose Line Is It Anyway?* hosted by Drew Carey, "where everything's made up and the points don't matter."

When improv actors perform, it seems almost magical how well they communicate. And it's *not* magic. They are following a strict set of rules called the rules of improv. Two of those rules are to make your partner look good and accept offers. These rules work together to keep the improvised conversations flowing smoothly until one of the actors can land a funny punchline.

Highlighting areas of agreement is the workplace equivalent of making your partner look good and accepting offers.

3. BE A HELPFUL COACH

Allow me to say something that might make you uncomfortable. You are deeply, fundamentally biased in almost everything you do. Don't worry, I'm not judging you personally. It's just part of how your brain works due to your **schemas: the mental frameworks governing how you interpret and respond to input.**

In the simplest terms, a schema is a lens that colors everything you see and do. It affects you in dozens of subtle ways, like your body posture, how quickly you smile, and the way you pause between words. Your schema also affects whether you assume the best or the worst of your employees.

Here's why this matters. Your brain always has at least one schema in play, whether you want to or not. In other words, you are always biased in one way or another.

The danger is that if you aren't paying attention, you might have inadvertently adopted a schema with a harmful bias. Doing so with your strong performers will destroy the flow of your conversations.

Fortunately, you aren't a slave to whatever schema your brain happens to be using at the time. You can change your schema by making a conscious effort to reframe the way you see the situation.

To keep the conversation flowing, consciously adopt the schema of a helpful coach giving feedback to a strong performer who is traveling a journey toward excellence.

A helpful coach is there to listen, ask thoughtful questions, and inspire the employee toward success. They are genuinely interested in helping the employee to succeed. They believe that strong performers consistently add value, help the team succeed, and work hard to make significant contributions.

Thinking of yourself as a helpful coach will change how you see your employees. It's another paradigm shift, like when you learned to think of your employees as strong performers.

It will cause you to be less aggressive, more patient, and more open. It will even increase trust. This leads to more positive interactions, agreement, and thoughtful patience. All of this helps to keep your conversations flowing.

Personally, I have found adopting a helpful coach schema only takes a few moments. Start with a slow, deep breath. Remind yourself that you're talking to a strong performer. Then visualize yourself as a helpful coach. Your brain will take it from there.

> Whether you like it or not, you always have at least one mental schema in play, at all times. Instead of trying to convince yourself that you aren't biased, try to adopt a bias that makes you a more effective people manager.
>
> For example, the book *Crucial Conversations: Tools for Talking When the Stakes Are High* by Kerry Patterson et al. offers "master my stories" and "start with heart," two tools for changing your schema.
>
> There are lots of schemas to choose from. For example, "I'm the official representative for senior leadership," "I'm a professional who acts with thoughtful purpose," or "I help others excel." You may recognize that last schema as one of my personal expectations from the expectations activity.

4. ASK OPEN-ENDED QUESTIONS

Are you getting one-word answers from your employees? If so, it's possible you're asking the wrong types of questions. Try asking open-ended questions that can only be answered by having a conversation.

Here's a simple refresher about the types of questions.

Type of Question	Discussion	Examples
Direct	Requires a "yes" or a "no" answer. Can be answered with almost no thought. Use only when you are absolutely sure you need a yes/no answer.	"Are we still meeting today?" "Do you have everything you need?" "Are you joining us for lunch?"
Specific	Requires a concise answer like "cold," "Tuesday," or "Pink." Limits thinking. When used back-to-back makes conversations feel like interrogations. Useful occasionally, when you need a specific answer.	"When would you like to meet again?" "Who will take point on that?"
Open ended	Requires a conversational answer. Promotes deep thinking. Reinforces that it is safe to share concerns. The bread and butter of one-on-ones.	"What else is on your mind?" "What's your plan for this? "What questions, thoughts, or concerns do you have?"

Allow me to address another elephant in the room. You probably have responsibilities for individual work in addition to managing your employees. You have a lot to do and limited time to do it.

As a result, you will be tempted to ask specific and direct questions. They seem simpler, faster. The key word here is "*seem*." In reality, they waste time by eliciting irrelevant facts. You end up playing "Twenty Questions" while missing what's most important.

Conversely, open-ended questions invite participation. They paint a more complete picture in less time because they keep the conversation flowing. Open-ended questions can also reveal root causes that would have remained hidden otherwise.

Open-ended questions are faster *in the long run*. That's why they teach this technique to doctors in medical school.

Consider the time-honored wrap-up, "Any questions?" This closed question invites a yes or no answer. It causes the receiver to consider two things. First, they must think of questions they might have. Second, they must decide how many of those questions are worth asking in front of other people. Usually, the answer is zero.

A better wrap-up is "What are your questions?" Better still, "What thoughts, questions, or concerns do you have?" And best of all, pause for a full fifteen seconds, making it clear that you believe there are thoughts, questions, or concerns that need to be shared.

5. STOP ASKING "WHY" QUESTIONS

"Why" questions are judgmental. When you ask your employee why they did something, you are implying that they have already failed. This triggers a defensive posture that decreases sharing and learning. It's the opposite of making it safe.

Here are some alternatives to "why" questions:

Don't Ask This	Ask This
"Why are you upset?"	"Tell me your thoughts."
"Why did you do that?"	"Wait. I think I might be confused. Can you help me understand what happened?"
"Why were you late again?"	"Yesterday, we discussed the importance of being on time. Talk to me."

"Why" questions turn conversations into fights. They replace understanding with blame. They make sharing feel dangerous. In other words, they prevent you from learning what your employees aren't telling you.

6. STOP ARGUING THE DETAILS

The sixth technique for keeping the conversation flowing is my second example of what *not* to do. Stop arguing about minor details. For clarity, "argue" means to quarrel with a person or to discuss something in a non-friendly way.

Arguing with your employees is as unproductive as a kayaker fighting a fast-flowing river. It is inefficient, damages your relationship, and is both physically and mentally exhausting. Arguing minor details brings conversations to a halt, raises the tension, and prevents you from learning what your employees aren't telling you.

In addition, arguing with your employees implies a fundamental misunderstanding of the power dynamic. Remember, *you* have higher status. If you absolutely want your employee to do it your way, then just say so. They report to you, not the other way around.

It's hard to justify ever arguing with your strong performers. After all, strong performers are good at their jobs. You value them. And the odds are good they are at least partially right.

We've been exploring the third question, "What aren't your

employees telling you?" In the last chapter, we discussed how to make it safe. In this chapter, I offered six techniques to keep your conversations flowing.

Technique	Discussion
Use the phrase "Tell me more."	Creates openness, keeps the conversation flowing, and invites your employee to share what's most important. These three words are almost magical.
Highlight areas of agreement.	Leverages the science of positive interactions to strengthen the relationship. Establishes a shared pool of understanding about the things you agree on.
Be a helpful coach.	Switches your mental schema to remind yourself that you are coaching a strong performer. This ensures your subconscious brain is helping you instead of hurting you.
Ask open-ended questions.	Invites broad participation. Creates space for your employee to engage with sensitive topics. It's the best question type for gathering lots of information quickly.
Stop asking "why" questions.	Reduces the judgment that triggers fear, raises tension, and shuts down conversations. Asking "Why?" makes the conversation less safe.
Stop arguing the details.	Reminds you to focus on the big picture instead of arguing over details that shut down your conversations. Be a leader—decide what's most important and use your influence to focus on that.
???	???

We're not quite done yet. I've saved the best for last. The seventh technique to keep the conversation flowing is so profoundly effective, it's earned an entire chapter all to itself.

Chapter 15

Banish "But"

Can I break the fourth wall for a moment? Some people picked up this book, hoping it would make them a better manager in five minutes. By getting this far, you've demonstrated grit, perseverance, and a commitment to travel a leadership journey that leads to greatness. That makes me happy for two reasons. First, it means I get to help you excel. Second, it means I can now share my super-secret superpower with you!

Banishing the word "but" will make you more effective in every conversation you ever have—for the rest of your life.

Let's start with the basics. In theory, "but" is used as a conjunction to contrast the statement before it to the statement that comes after. It's meant to create a relative comparison.

- This tree is tall enough, *but* that one is too small.
- Friendly *but* quiet.

In practice, "but" is used to give the barest minimum acknowledgement while simultaneously diminishing the importance of whatever was just said. "But" is more like a sword meant to slash your opponent's words.

- "I hear what you're saying, *but* we don't have the time."
- "It's a nice idea, *but* we already tried that."
- "Yes, *but...*"

The truth is that "but" *cancels* everything that comes before it. Whatever comes after the "but" is the *real* message.

Now, here's the problem. If you are like most people, then you use the word "but" dozens of times a day. And each time you do, you are chipping away at trust.

The Harm of "But"	Discussion
Prevents conversations from flowing smoothly	Using "but" is like fighting the river instead of flowing with it. "But" signals that you are in a verbal battle to argue your point, which can shift your schema and your employee's schema into a bad place.
Leads to intense, negative interactions	Using "but" negates your attempts to leverage positive feedback. In other words, it cancels out the positive benefits of everything in Chapter 11—the laws of learning (intensity plus effect), the five-to-one rule, and the incentive theory of motivation.
Cancels *your own* words	Using "but" on your own statements cancels what *you* just said. It reduces *trust* that your words matter, obscures your true message, and wastes people's time.
Makes it less safe	"But" feels like a rejection, even if you had good intentions. That reduces psychological safety, which prevents you from discovering what's important.

"But" is a habit. You probably use it all the time without thinking about it. It's a *bad* habit worth breaking. Let me show you why with a personal story.

MY INDIE ADVENTURE

Years ago, I started a little Indie studio that I ran in my spare time. I built short story-based apps that I'd sell in app stores.

Five nights a week, I'd write, edit, and rewrite my stories. On Saturday, I'd ask my wife for feedback, which often went like this:

> She would say, "I liked it, *but* some parts rambled. The intro could be shorter, and I don't understand the part about the dog. *But* it was good."

Her response was a textbook example of bad feedback. It was vague, full of "buts," and hard to act on. More importantly, it crushed my self-confidence.

This was before I had learned about the growth mindset, so I was still struggling with the fixed mindset. What I heard was "Your story stinks. You're not good enough. You are a failure." And every time she gave me this kind of feedback, despite her sincere desire to help, I walked away thinking, *I can't do this. This is too hard.*

Then one day, my wife shared a new communication tool she had learned at work: "Yes, and..." You start by replacing the word "but" with "and." Next, you provide positive reinforcement about some part of what was said (a.k.a. the "yes"). Finally, you make small, specific suggestions for their consideration.

The next Saturday, we decided to give "yes, and..." a try. I shared my latest story and asked again for feedback. This time, my wife paused for several minutes before responding. I stood there waiting, fidgeting. I shuffled my feet.

> She said, "I really liked it. In fact, I felt like I was reliving that moment. I could feel the passion and the pain you experienced, like I was right there. It was powerful. *And* I think it could be *even stronger* if you removed the paragraph about the dog, trimmed a few sentences right after the introduction, and cut a few words in the last paragraph to make it snappier."

My wife had assumed the schema of a helpful coach. She didn't just say she liked it. She highlighted that she'd felt the passion, remembered the pain, and relived the moment.

Then she used the potent words, "even stronger," which, as you learned earlier, was a way of reminding me that she thought of me as a strong performer. Finally, she suggested clear, specific guidance that I could act on.

My wife's second attempt at giving feedback included a big "YES" and a little "and" that strongly emphasized areas of agreement and added specific ways my work could be even stronger. This felt entirely different than the previous week's feedback.

Instead of feeling discouraged, I was filled with energy, optimism, and a deep enthusiasm to make my story even stronger.

And all of this happened even though I knew exactly what she was doing.

Allow me to break the fourth wall one last time. Those people who skimmed the book never got to hear this story. They will never understand that this experience changed my life. It is why "YES AND" became one of only two personalized license plates in my entire life. It was such a powerful moment, that right now, as I type this more than a decade later, I have goosebumps running up and down my arms.

THE LESSON

After experiencing the power of "yes, and..." firsthand, I set about removing "but" from my vocabulary. I tried to never, ever use it again, even when it intuitively (habitually) seemed like the right word to use. In the spirit of banishing "but," I also banished similar expressions like "however" and "except."

Listen. I've been teaching management workshops for years. Many of my participants already know my reputation as a good communicator. They've often collaborated with my teams. Sometimes they've even personally heard me navigate difficult conversations.

When I teach them to banish "but," I see connections firing in their minds. It's an epic light-bulb moment. They realize they've just learned a secret that's been hiding in plain sight all along.

Banishing "but" is my not-so-secret-anymore superpower. It increases psychological safety, keeps conversations flowing, and helps me discover the information I need to lead my teams to success.

It's simple, in theory. Stop saying the words "but," "however," and "except." Of course, simple doesn't mean easy. There are decades of learned, habitual patterns that include those three words.

Here's how I broke those bad habits:

1. Replace "but" with "and."
2. Replace "but" with a short pause (or a period).
3. Cut everything before the "but."
4. Start over.

After one of my "yes, and" workshops, an employee said to me, "I see your point, but..." Then she corrected herself, "*And*...sometimes it feels sort of fake. Like we're sprinkling in sincerity." Her point was both insightful and ironic. What I heard was "insincerity," not "in sincerity." Being insincere is one of the surest ways to destroy trust. So, as you start to banish "but," make sure that you're not sprinkling insincerity into your conversations.

1. REPLACE "BUT" WITH "AND"

If you pay attention, you will notice you often use "but" as a way to increase the drama or make your point seem more important. Neither of those is necessary when you are talking with your employees, especially in a one-on-one.

Try replacing the word "but" with the word "and." Swapping the two words allows the part before and after to both be true. It can be used in most situations. It's also surprisingly effective.

I've used "but" instead of "and" in dozens of places throughout this book. Here's just one example from Chapter 1:

- "They can make assumptions. They can infer. *And* they cannot know for sure."

If I had used "but," it would have minimized the danger of assumptions. Instead, the "and" reinforced that all three things could be true at the same time. That reinforced what I was trying to teach.

> Most people notice right away that they use "but" to cancel other people's statements. It takes them longer to realize they also use "but" to cancel their own statements. For example, "I was stuck but not really stuck. In fact, I had an idea for how to solve the problem, but I still wasn't sure." When you "but" yourself, you create awkward, hard-to-follow conversations that cause your listener to lose faith that your words matter. Don't "but" yourself.

2. REPLACE "BUT" WITH A SHORT PAUSE (OR A PERIOD)

The second technique is helpful when two statements might be slightly in opposition. Replace "but" with a short pause when speaking; in text, replace it with a period or start a new paragraph.

The pause (or period) allows each statement to stand on its own, without canceling either one. It also helps to separate the ideas.

Like the first technique, I've used this in many places throughout this book. Here's just one example from Chapter 2:

- "My engagement skyrocketed. My performance increased. The only difference was that I now knew what was expected of me."

Instead of starting that third sentence with "But," the period allows the prior two statements to remain true while also reinforcing that I'm switching to a new idea. For a bigger break, I could have started a new paragraph.

This technique is even more effective while speaking. A short pause makes it clear there are two distinct ideas. A long pause allows you to switch directions entirely, without canceling what you already said.

As a side benefit, using a pause while speaking gives your listener a moment to catch up. It will also make you seem more charismatic. Win-win!

Never, ever use the expression "but anyway." It tells your listener that everything you've just said has been a complete waste of their time. At best, it implies you are distractible. At worst, it implies you don't know what you want to say. In all cases, it decreases trust that your words matter.

3. CUT EVERYTHING BEFORE THE "BUT"

If you can't just replace "but" with "and," and inserting a period isn't working out, then take a moment to think. Be honest with yourself. Make sure you aren't setting up a false comparison, adding unnecessary drama, or constructing a straw man argument.

If you are, then quit it. Cut the junk you had before the "but." Then focus on your actual point.

Remember, you are almost always working with a strong performer, in which case, there's no need for all that drama. So take a moment to regroup. Figure out what you are trying to say. Then make your actual point without all the preamble.

It won't take you long to realize that you don't need the garbage before the "but." It's not as dramatic as your brain wants you to think it is. And it causes real harm.

I can't point you to an example of this in my writing because I did not use "but," "however," or "except" anywhere else in this book.

4. START OVER

The final technique to banish "but" is a special case of the previous technique.

Sometimes, when you are writing a document or preparing a presentation, you can get to a point where you feel you absolutely need that "but," "however," or "except." It seems critical to driving home your message.

From my experience, this usually means you are trying to create a big, dramatic moment with a pivotal "but!" Worse, it sometimes means you don't really know what you're trying to say. Either way, it's unnecessary.

My advice is to start over, this time without the "but." Slow down, step away from the text, and come back to it later when you're fresh. As a leader with influence, your words matter. Figure out what you *really* want to say. Then say that!

> If I find myself typing "but," that's a warning sign that I'm emotionally triggered. Typing while triggered has never ended well for me. Eventually, I came up with a rule—never hit "send" while emotional. Step away, sleep on it, and start over the next day.

A one-on-one is not the time for dramatic, courtroom-style antics. Keep the conversation flowing. Increase psychological safety. Find out what your employees aren't telling you.

Said another way, use these tools in your one-on-ones to discuss what's most important:

- Make it safe.
  - Be present.
  - Use active listening.
  - Be vulnerable.
  - Admit fallibility.
  - State it explicitly.
- Keep the conversation flowing.
  - Use the phrase "Tell me more."
  - Highlight areas of agreement.
  - Be a helpful coach.
  - Ask open-ended questions.
  - Stop asking "why" questions.
  - Stop arguing the details.
  - Banish "but."

Practice these if you want to be a good manager. Master them if you want to be a great one.

Part 4

ARE YOUR EMPLOYEES HIGHLY ENGAGED?

Chapter 16

Increase Engagement

I've got news to share. It's sort of a good news—bad news—good news sandwich.

The first slice of good news? You've come a really long way. You know how to clarify expectations for your employees. You know how to provide helpful, positive feedback to your strong performers. And you've learned to make it safe and keep the conversation flowing.

The slice of bad news? The answer to the fourth question, "Are your employees highly engaged?" is still "Probably not." Studies by Gallup show that less than 40 percent of U.S. employees self-report as highly engaged.

Fortunately, there is another slice of good news. Seventy percent of the variance in employee engagement is attributable to their people manager.

Now, build your sandwich. Good news: you are stronger than

you were. Bad news: many of your employees are not highly engaged. Good news: as a strong people manager, you can do something about it. You have an opportunity to make a real difference.

WHAT IS ENGAGEMENT?

Engagement is not the same thing as happiness, emotional well-being, or even having clear expectations. Engagement is about *commitment.*

An engaged employee is *committed* to doing great work. This commitment manifests itself in hundreds of ways, large and small. Engaged employees:

- Work harder to create better products.
- Are more proactive toward anticipating future problems.
- Are more driven to create success for their teams, products, and customers.
- Demonstrate more perseverance in the face of setbacks.
- Are more motivated, mindful of critical details, and willing to make themselves stronger.

A highly engaged employee is more valuable in every way that matters. And a team of highly engaged employees can handle just about anything!

Want some data? Forbes, Gallup, Fortune, and others have reported that companies with highly engaged employees have:

- 20 percent increased profitability
- 15 percent increased productivity per employee
- 40–80 percent lower absenteeism
- 70 percent fewer safety incidents
- 55 percent less turnover of employees

Highly engaged employees have a huge financial impact, leading to more profit, increased productivity, and higher retention.

THE VALUE OF ENGAGEMENT

To show what high engagement looks like in practice, consider what happened when several of my highly engaged teams experienced a critical failure that jeopardized three months of work worth tens of millions of dollars.

I shared the problem with the entire team. "Due to some confusion on our part, the deadline we thought was in three weeks is actually just three days from now."

I asked for their thoughts. Then I just listened. After some back and forth, one of my leaders spoke up: "I don't think we should ask for an extension. In fact, I think we can finish in three days."

From there, they began discussing how we could finish the project in the next three days. They collaborated, created a plan, and made sure everyone had a chance to voice their concerns. Three days later, we released the product with zero defects!

No one cast blame, argued, or worked overtime. Instead, a group of highly engaged employees rose to meet this new challenge, weeks ahead of our original timeline.

To understand how they succeeded, you'd have to go back three months to when the project started. That's when I (and other leaders) did all the things I've been talking about in this book. We clarified expectations, made it safe to raise concerns, and praised the behaviors that would lead to success.

Said simpler, we used our influence to increase engagement.

As a result, every team member was committed to success. They fearlessly raised issues, removed barriers, and collaborated to solve problems I wasn't even aware of until after the fact. They did this for two straight months so that by the time our schedule was cut short, they were practically done.

> The flip side of high engagement is low engagement. Low engagement means low commitment. It manifests as a lack of professionalism, inconsistent or low performance, and interpersonal conflicts. Low engagement decreases speed, creative problem-solving, and quality. It's also the root cause of quiet quitting, when disengagement leads an employee to do the bare minimum (a.k.a. "coasting").

INCREASING ENGAGEMENT

Guess what? You already know how to increase engagement. We've been talking about it all along. Let me show you what I mean.

Topic	Impact on Engagement
Expectations	Knowing what's expected is the number one predictor of engagement. Use the expectations activity and revisit it periodically.
Confusion	Confusion eats away at commitment. Use your influence to remove it. Check for understanding, use not-just-any-rock, and slow down to speed up.
Leadership style	Adopting the right leadership style (directing, coaching, supporting, or empowering) can increase mastery and autonomy, which are key drivers of engagement.
Disengagement	The feedback tools from Chapter 8 can also help: look for root causes, remove blockers, and focus on personal growth.
Strong performers	Treating your employees as strong performers helps them feel valued, increases autonomy, and increases engagement. Use the five-to-one rule—even better, create twenty positives for each negative, or drop the one negative altogether.
Growth mindset	The growth mindset also increases engagement. Use growth-oriented language that emphasizes learning, growing, and overcoming.
Praise behaviors	Praising behaviors is a powerful way to increase engagement. It clarifies what's important, invokes the law of effect (a.k.a. positivity), and promotes both real mastery and the perception of mastery.
Law of intensity	Intense situations help you learn faster with higher motivation. Because negative intensity invites unintended consequences, use positive intensity to increase engagement.
Make it safe	Psychological safety also helps with engagement. Be present, ask clarifying questions that invite participation, recap decisions, and admit fallibility.
Keep the conversation flowing	Being part of the conversation increases a person's engagement. Use tools such as "Tell me more," highlighting areas of agreement, and open-ended questions. And, of course, banish "but" (and embrace big YES, little and).

In his book *Drive*, Daniel Pink provides wonderful insights about engagement. As he explains, there are three primary drivers of engagement: autonomy, mastery, and purpose. Autonomy is an employee's ability to direct significant aspects of their work. Mastery refers to the employee's skill, knowledge, or prior successes. Purpose is the employee's belief that their work has value. If you want to increase engagement, use your influence to help your employee increase autonomy, mastery, or purpose. Better yet, increase all three!

Now that you know why engagement matters and how to increase it, you'll need an easy way to track it so you will know when to do something about it.

Chapter 17

Engagement Activity

Staffing is a long game. So, too, is employee engagement. It starts before the employee is hired, spikes during the "honeymoon phase," and then waxes and wanes for the duration of their employment.

Because engagement is constantly changing, you need a way to assess it. The engagement activity is a two-step process for assessing employee engagement:

1. Ask your employee to rate their engagement on a scale from one to ten.
2. Find out what their answer means.

This is one of my favorite activities, and it's hard to get wrong.

1. ASKING THE QUESTION

Start by asking your employee how they would rate their current level of engagement with their work on a scale of one to ten. When you ask the question, give it some context to help your employee understand what you mean. For example:

"On a scale of one to ten, where one means 'I hate my job; I dread coming to work each day,' and ten means 'I love my job; I look forward to my work each day,' how would you describe your level of engagement with your work right now?"

The one-to-ten scale is less threatening than an open-ended question. It makes it easier to track engagement over time. And it sets the stage for a deeper conversation in step 2.

This ten-point scale is particularly effective when engagement is low. Remember, you are threatening—it's less scary for your employee to say "five" than "I'm not engaged with my work."

Practically speaking, most employees will give a number between four and ten. In my experience, eight or nine is great; six or below is bad; and seven is dangerous. Of course, these are just guidelines.

What's important is that the number oscillates. It waxes and wanes depending on team makeup, projects, and differences in tasks from one day to the next. This variability is amplified because employees like some parts of the work more than others. In addition, their engagement can be affected by things outside of work, like family, health, or world events.

Oscillating engagement means that you have to be watchful. A bad week can drop engagement by one or two points. That's why I consider a seven to be dangerous.

The perfect ten generally requires three conditions: your employee loves their current tasks, they're in sync with their teammates, and they are happy with their personal life outside of work.

A perfect ten is wonderful, rare, and worth savoring. It's also temporary. Don't expect it to last, and don't worry when it passes.

With all of that said, the number itself isn't actually all that important. That's because it's relative, subjective, and often, unreliable. That's why there's a second step to the engagement activity.

2. FIND OUT WHAT THEIR ANSWER MEANS

Asking for the number is just the first step. After your employee gives you a number, follow up to learn more about what that number means to them. Find out what motivates your employee, which aspects of their work they do or don't like, and what's impacting their engagement.

Use the number they give you to switch to big, open-ended questions like these:

1. "What does the work feel like when your engagement is a seven?"
2. "What keeps it from dropping to a six?"
3. "What kind of work are you doing when it's an eight?"
4. "What would a nine look like?"

Each question attacks the problem from a different direction, depending on what you want to learn. If your employee seems highly engaged, explore what they are enjoying. That will help you create even more of those moments in the future.

If engagement is low right now, find out which kind of work they enjoyed before. Look for what's getting in the way, which work seems boring, or whether they have conflicts with other team members. Discover whether they lack mastery, autonomy, or purpose. Look for opportunities to create personal growth.

From my experience, there's really no wrong way to do the second step. Just make it safe, keep the conversation flowing, and learn whatever you can. That will make it possible to use your influence to increase engagement.

MEET KAMILLE

Let me show you how the engagement activity played out with one of my soft-spoken employees. Kamille had a reserved demeanor that made it hard to discover what he was really thinking.

When I asked Kamille the engagement question, he hesitated for a long time before answering, "Maybe a seven." This gave me pause. After all, a seven could quickly become a six or a five. More importantly, Kamille generally seemed to like his work.

I suspected there was more to his story.

"Okay, maybe a seven. What kinds of things are you doing when it's an eight?"

Kamille paused, "I really enjoyed working on the animations a few weeks ago."

"Tell me more."

"Implementing the animations was challenging—nailing the timing, iterating with the designers, helping the artists. I felt like part of the creative process."

This was the first time Kamille had ever mentioned the "creative process." After a few more minutes of exploration, I learned that while he loved being part of the creative process, he wasn't taking on those kinds of tasks as often as he could. Kamille assumed everyone else wanted to be a part of the creative process too. He didn't want to be selfish.

After this profound discovery, I revisited the expectations activity with Kamille. By the end of our one-on-one, Kamille had crafted a new expectation: "Pick tasks that are part of the creative process."

When I checked in a few months later, Kamille reported a nine in engagement!

Incredible! Even more so because he'd stayed on the same team, continued working on the same project, and had the same overall assignment. What changed was Kamille's sense of autonomy and the clear expectation that he must advocate for himself. With that, his engagement sky-rocketed.

I made this happen. I used my influence to discover what kind of work was most engaging to Kamille and then captured that in his expectations.

Kamille's commitment went from a seven all the way up to a nine. And he stayed there for years. This was a perfect example of how people managers account for *positive* variance in employee engagement.

What you do matters. Use the engagement activity to learn more about your employee's motivations. Then use your influence to make a difference in any way you can.

> The video games industry is ultra-competitive. Other studios are constantly poaching our strong performers, even the junior employees with little experience. Our competitors send emails offering more money, glitzy projects, and promotions. And with the new reality of remote work, competition for my staff is now global. To combat that, I try to keep engagement so high—at an eight, nine, or ten—that my employees never even open our competitors' recruiting emails!

HOW OFTEN?

Sometimes managers ask me how often they should use the engagement activity. Ironically, it's possible to use the engagement activity both too often and too infrequently.

When used too often, an employee may begin anticipating that you will ask about their engagement. This leads some employees to pre-craft false narratives that protect their vulnerabilities. Yes, that really happens.

When used too infrequently, you risk an employee's engagement dropping drastically while you weren't paying attention. You might not notice the decline before they're handing in their resignation.

Generally, I recommend using the engagement activity when something changes, if an employee says something that doesn't feel quite right, or periodically, as a way to check in.

It's also a nice way to kick off your one-on-one if you don't have anything pressing to discuss.

The engagement activity helps you take the pulse of your employee's engagement. It also helps you discover what's most important if you don't already know. Plus, it gives you a simple way to track engagement over time. That helps with the long game.

The engagement activity isn't hard to do, and generally, it's hard to do wrong. That's why it's one of my favorites.

And now that you know how to track engagement, let's dig deeper into the root causes of low engagement—the three Cs.

Chapter 18

The Three Cs

Confusion is often the root cause of low engagement. Let me show you what I mean.

Imagine the start of the year at Acme Widgets. Sally, who was recently promoted to team lead, had new ideas for how her team could help Acme deliver more products this year. Specifically, Sally believed her engineers were perfectly situated to identify overall bottlenecks in Acme's process. Sally had an ambitious plan to help the entire company!

She started her "New Year's Kickoff" meeting with tons of energy. After a nice motivational speech, she said, "*We* need to deliver *sooner.*" Sally then moved on, talking about how her initiative would work, and how everyone could contribute.

Also in that meeting was "Meets Expectations" Joe. By this time, Joe had mostly gotten over his end-of-year rating. He was trying to start the new year on the right foot. Then he heard Sally say, "*You* need to work *faster.*"

He was shocked to hear this from Sally, of all people. She seemed like a quality-over-quantity kind of person. Joe sort of zoned out for a minute, so he missed a few of the details. Then Sally moved on to the next topic.

Joe went home that night feeling confused. He began telling himself stories. Sally's promotion had gone to her head. He thought back over everything Sally had ever said. Maybe she'd always been like this.

Joe's confusion morphed into concern. And when mixed with his prior irritation over his end-of-year rating, his concern festered, until eventually, Joe erupted in the middle of a meeting, causing a huge conflict.

THE THREE Cs

Seeing this situation, you might be wondering, "How was Sally supposed to know Joe was confused?" And that's the crux of the matter. It was Sally's job, as his manager, to uncover Joe's confusion. It was also her job to remove that confusion.

Confusion is not a minor inconvenience. It is the root cause of most major problems. Simple misunderstandings evolve into deeper confusion. Confusion evolves into concern. And concern can fester until it triggers significant conflict.

Even if confusion doesn't evolve into concern or conflict, it's still bad. Confusion is often a major contributor to low performance. Plus, it can destroy engagement.

Sally could have moved toward the confusion, concern, or conflict (the three Cs). I think of this as three separate steps:

1. **Watch.** Be vigilant for any sign of confusion, concern, or conflict. Use proactive measures to check for confusion, including the tools in Chapter 8: Your Employee Is Confused and Chapter 13: Active Listening.

2. **Decide.** Once you sense something isn't right, make a concrete decision about when and how you will act. This is where many managers fail. To remind yourself to do this, consider adding it to your leadership vision (see Chapter 7: Walk the Walk).

3. **Act.** Have the courage to remove the confusion, address the concern, or approach the conflict before engagement is destroyed. Try using the tools in Part 3: What Aren't Your Employees Telling You?

These steps might happen in quick succession in the moment. Or they might be spread out over hours or even days. Your action will vary depending on which C you're dealing with:

- **Confusion.** Confusion is common. Assume it exists, especially when something is changing. Ask questions, use recaps, and explore new topics from multiple angles. If you detect confusion, address it immediately. This is particularly effective in one-on-ones, where you have time to move slowly. Even if time is short, or if you're in a larger setting, it's still best to address confusion right away. After all, if one person is confused, others are too.

- **Concern.** When people are concerned, they often tell themselves stories to explain what's happening. Overnight, their stories become bigger, broader, and harder to address. If possible, try to address concerns within a few hours. While confusion is common in large groups, concerns are often unique to each individual. It's generally better to address concerns in small groups or one-on-ones.

- **Conflict.** Serious conflict evokes strong emotions that can escalate into a physical confrontation—that's outside the scope of this book. For run-of-the-mill conflicts between employees, it's helpful to wait overnight to allow emotions to settle before attempting a resolution. Then, make it safe (Chapter 13) and keep the conversation flowing (Chapter 14). Also, consider reading *Crucial Conversations* by Patterson et al. You can prevent most conflicts from ever happening by using the tools you've already learned, if you act early enough.

The three Cs are all bad. And they get worse over time, if left to fester. That's where you come in. Use your influence to prevent confusion from evolving into concern, and concern from escalating into conflict. The sooner you do this, the easier it will be.

Don't "wait and see" with the three Cs.

Moving toward the three Cs is a simple tool. Unfortunately, I had to learn it the hard way. That's why I can relate to Sally.

Sally was new to being a team leader. She made two rookie mistakes: 1) assuming she was being perfectly clear and

2) assuming no one had concerns with the new plan. My younger self made those same mistakes.

Any time a team pivots, there's going to be confusion. There's no way around it. So, no matter how fast you need to make a change, take the time to slow down, invite active discussion, and check for full understanding. Said simpler, slow down to speed up.

It's impossible to prevent concern, confusion, and conflict from ever happening. That's not the goal. The goal is to *watch* for the three Cs, *decide* to act, and *take action*.

As bad as the three Cs can be, they aren't the worst challenge you'll face as a people manager. Sometimes, your employee is really and truly a low performer, hence our final question.

Part 5

WHAT ABOUT LOW PERFORMERS?

Chapter 19

Impact of Low Performers

You've come so far! You know how to set expectations, give feedback, and figure out what your employees aren't telling you. If you are using what you've learned, you should be seeing higher engagement, and ultimately, higher performance.

Now, it's finally time to tackle the feedback scenario I've been putting off since Chapter 8. It's time to answer the question, "What about low performers?"

First, let's revisit the definition. A low performer adds little value, harms the overall team, or fails to meet the minimum expectations for their title.

A low performer might be floundering with core work, struggling to achieve the basic professionalism required by your company, or falling short in team collaboration. Whatever the shortcoming, having a low performer is a serious situation that you must address.

WARNING SIGNS

In my experience, low performers often go unnoticed for far too long. It happens because it's hard to know exactly when an employee officially becomes a low performer. It happens because we all want our employees to succeed, and because it's hard to tell someone they aren't doing a good job.

Whatever the reason, the result is the same. Most managers fail to take action until it becomes egregious. Don't be like most managers. Pay attention to the warning signs.

Warning Sign	Discussion
Confusion	While confusion is common, it's a sign of a low performer when an employee's confusion becomes extreme, persists despite your efforts, or occurs frequently. Low performers will routinely be confused, even when the rest of your team seems to understand.
Lacking knowledge/skill	While no employee is great at everything, a low performer is often seriously deficient in essential knowledge/skills. They often struggle to grasp how much they need to improve. If you are paying attention, you will notice that they work slowly, demonstrate poor quality, or are incapable of doing the work without significant help.
Low engagement	Prolonged periods of disengagement are another warning sign of a low performer. Watch for clues that they are demotivated, disinterested, or disgruntled. Low performers will often hide this from you, so you will have to look carefully.

These warning signs match three of the five feedback scenarios from Chapter 8: How Do You Give Feedback? When I introduced those three scenarios, it was from the perspective that you were working with a strong performer. That's why I shared tools for mitigating confusion, lack of knowledge/skill, and low engagement.

If those tools only made marginal improvements, then the three scenarios now become warning signs of a bigger problem. Your employee may be drifting into dangerously low performance.

If the scenarios persist, you will need to determine the employee's capability and willingness, as follows:

1. The low performer is *incapable* of becoming a strong performer.
2. The low performer is *unwilling* to become a strong performer.
3. The low performer is both *capable* of becoming a strong performer and is *willing* to work hard to do so (in a timely fashion).

Determining that your employee is both capable and willing will require an entirely different approach. You'll need to set aside some of the tools you learned earlier in this book. You'll also need to learn a few new tools.

Managing a low performer requires another paradigm shift in your thinking. To understand why, let's look at the harm a low performer can cause.

Some of the tools you will use with low performers are harsh. Before using them, take a pause. Make sure what you're seeing is not just a routine, minor deviation in performance that could be addressed with the tools covered in earlier chapters. Be certain it's a serious deficiency that meets your definition of a low performer.

THE HARM

A team is more than the sum of its parts—it's not simply A + B + C + D. This is because most people don't work in a vacuum. They talk to each other, solve (or create) problems for each other, and impact each other's work.

Employees are force multipliers; they affect everyone else's productivity.

Strong performers *enhance* other employees' productivity. They share knowledge and best practices, work together to solve problems, and provide assistance with each other's work. The effect is multiplicative, as in, A * B * C * D. Strong performers make the whole team stronger. Hence the expression, "The whole is greater than the sum of its parts."

In contrast, low performers *diminish* other employees' productivity. Low performers make conversations harder; they create problems instead of solving them; and they negatively impact other people's work. Low performers are often the bottleneck in processes. In addition, their work requires extra oversight, guidance, or iteration from your strong performers, which takes time.

Like strong performers, the impact of a low performer is also multiplicative, in this case, in a bad way. As a result, a low performer can harm nearly every aspect of the work, making the whole team weaker.

Impact of a Low Performer	Discussion
Decreases productivity	It's a double-whammy—the low performer contributes less than expected themselves, plus they reduce the productivity of your strong performers.
Impairs collaboration	A low performer introduces distractions, disruptions, and breakdowns in communication. This makes team interactions slower and less clear.
Compromises team trust	As we learned in Chapter 1, trust requires capabilities and results, hence low performers are rarely trusted by their peers. Teams with low trust move slower—author Stephen M.R. Covey calls this the "trust tax."
Compromises trust in leadership	Left unchecked, low performers cause strong performers to lose trust in you as the people manager. Worse still, they may lose trust in the larger organization, wondering, "How come nobody does anything about that?"
Decreases psychological safety	Strong performers often feel bad about calling out others for low performance. This makes all conversations slightly less safe, especially for topics that even remotely relate to team performance.
Lowers morale	Strong performers inspire each other. Low performers do the opposite, discouraging other members of the team.
Reduces fairness	A strong performer may feel like a low performer isn't being held to the same standard. It doesn't seem fair.
Decreases engagement	Low performers create a cloud of confusion, concern, and conflict. They also reduce the engagement of your strong performers. If left unaddressed, this can cause your strong performers to look for another job.
Drains creativity	Low performers evoke strong, negative emotions in others. This reduces your team's energy, momentum, and creative problem-solving.

The impact of a low performer on an otherwise high-performing team is overwhelmingly negative. In many cases, your team would be better off without the low performer, even if it means having one less person on the team.

The longer a low performer is on your team, the larger the negative impact.

★ ★ ★

In addition to the impact to the team, low performers also impact you as the people manager.

Managing a low performer can be a soul-crushing experience. It often leads to self-doubt, second-guessing, and emotional angst. The experience can be so difficult that you will want to quit.

In severe cases, the process can be so emotionally distressing that it might even make you question whether you still want to be a people manager at all. I've seen this happen. I don't want it to happen to you.

I want you to learn how to deal with low performers. Because eventually you will have one on your team, no matter how hard you try.

So take a deep breath, roll up your sleeves, and let's discuss three techniques for managing low performers:

1. Make it clear
2. Know the rules
3. Prepare yourself

Chapter 20

Make It Clear

Low performers struggle to truly understand how bad things are. Consider this story of an employee I managed some time ago:

> Todd was unexpectedly transferred into my department. Unfortunately, he began struggling right away. I told him he needed to improve his speed, quality, and communication.
>
> Todd said he understood. Then he made a few minor improvements. Week after week, we had almost the same conversation. I told him he needed to improve, he said he understood, and he made tiny improvements.
>
> Eventually, I had to fire him. As I was walking him out of the building, Todd said, "I don't understand. I thought I was improving. I didn't realize I could lose my job."

I went back over my notes. I thought about our one-on-one conversations. I had been clear that his job was at risk. *Hadn't I?*

It took me a long time to come to terms with Todd's departing words. Eventually, I realized Todd never truly understood how bad his performance was, or that his job was at risk. He never perceived how serious the threat really was (per Maslow's hierarchy). As a result, Todd had less motivation to improve and no sense of urgency about it. He was basically doomed from the start.

My mistake with Todd was that I assumed I was being clear, when in fact, I was not. Let me explain where I went wrong.

Low performers often struggle with the **Dunning-Kruger effect, the tendency for people with low skill to be unaware of how unskilled they are.** The shorthand for this is, "unskilled and unaware."

Low performers aren't skilled enough to fully realize what makes strong performance possible. This makes it hard for them to truly understand how bad their own performance is, no matter how many hints, suggestions, or clues you drop. Furthermore, low performers are likely confused, lacking knowledge/skill, or disengaged, which makes it hard to appreciate that their job is at risk.

The result is less motivation, less urgency, and less improvement.

MAKE IT CLEAR

In the years that followed Todd's departure, I pushed myself to become a stronger people manager. Through trial and error, I devised six tools that ensure an employee understands the true extent of their low performance *and* that their job is at risk:

1. Don't soften the blow.
2. Use formal language.
3. Don't argue the details.
4. Be specific.
5. Confirm they understand.
6. Minimize praise (and other tools for strong performers).

1. DON'T SOFTEN THE BLOW

It feels awful to tell someone they are failing, and you have to do it anyway. Your employee needs to improve. They need to know that their job is at stake. Otherwise, there is little hope they will improve enough to keep their job.

Don't soften the blow. Avoid softening language which could be misinterpreted in any way. For example.

- "You are doing mostly okay."
- "You just need to improve a few things."
- "Everyone goes through tough spots."
- "You'll get through this."

Even though you will probably feel compelled to say supportive statements like this, don't. They will confuse your employee, which makes it more likely that they will lose their job.

2. USE FORMAL LANGUAGE

To make it clear, you must shatter the illusion that this is a run-of-the-mill conversation. Use precise, formal language when giving feedback to a low performer.

When I say "formal," I mean it. Spell out their title, team, and company. Explicitly use the designations from your end-of-year rating system: "below expectations" or "low performer." Then connect those terms to their performance and to the possible outcomes. For example:

> "Todd, you are currently a low performer as an engineer on the Alpha Team at Acme Widgets. Your performance must improve significantly for you to continue working in this role."

Practice what you're going to say in advance, several times. You're going to have to say these words more than once. Your message needs to be strong, clear, and consistent every time.

In the video games industry, we have an axiom, "If the player didn't see the feedback, then the feedback didn't happen." It doesn't matter how many colorful stars we send flying across the screen, how glaringly obvious the gold coins were, or how many sounds we play when you crash your car. If the player didn't notice the stars, coins, or sounds, then that feedback failed.

The same principle applies to managing a low performer; "If your employee doesn't understand the feedback, then the feedback didn't happen." That's why formal language matters.

3. DON'T ARGUE THE DETAILS

When you tell an employee they are a low performer, you are directly threatening their ability to provide for themselves and their family. According to Maslow's hierarchy (see Chapter 13), this is almost as threatening as a physical attack.

People respond to this threat in different ways. Some get quiet, focusing inward. Others get vocal, projecting outward. Most become defensive in some way. Almost everyone will ask for clarification, which is where many managers fall into a trap.

You might not have been clear when you asked for a certain report. Perhaps you were vague about your expectations. Or maybe another employee did the same thing without consequences. You may have created confusion by praising your employee just last week.

Don't fall into the trap of arguing about minor details.

When you get distracted by arguing the details, you enable the low performer to falsely believe they are "winning" the argument. You open the door for them to push back. This reduces their sense of urgency about the seriousness of the problem.

If you find yourself arguing, stop. Take a deep breath. Go back to the formal language:

> "While there are some details we could discuss, I want to be clear. Your recent performance makes you a low performer as an engineer on the Alpha Team at Acme Widgets. It's important that you understand that your job is at risk."

End all arguments by restating the formal language as many times as needed. This is why you practiced it earlier.

4. BE SPECIFIC

Switch your leadership style to that of directing. Be specific about which behaviors are deficient, how they need to improve, and what results need to be accomplished. Use simple, clear language.

Avoid the empowering or supporting leadership styles. Tell them exactly what needs to improve and how.

When talking about behaviors, avoid broad generalizations, such as "You're always late!" Broad generalizations are rarely 100 percent accurate. That opens the door to arguments about the details. Be specific:

> "Last week, you arrived late to three separate meetings. The week before, you completely missed two morning stand-ups. You need to be on time to all meetings going forward."

5. CONFIRM THEY UNDERSTAND

The fifth tool is going to feel uncomfortable. Unfortunately, it cannot be avoided.

Ask the low performer to repeat back to you the formal language you used in step two when you told them just how bad their performance has been and that their job is at risk. For example:

"Before we proceed, can you repeat back what I just said? I want to make sure I'm being absolutely clear."

This may take several attempts. After all, your employee is probably upset. In my experience they will be reluctant to say the formal words out loud. Instead, they'll use casual language like "Yes, I understand. I need to improve."

Casual language is not sufficient.

That's part of the mistake I made with Todd. It's part of the reason he was surprised when I eventually had to let him go. It's the same mistake I've seen almost every other manager make the first few times they had to oversee a low performer.

No matter how awkward it is, keep at it until your employee repeats back the formal language. It's the only way to be absolutely sure they understand, without equivocation, wiggle room, or ambiguity.

> Repeat Backs are a great tool for confirming understanding with your strong performers too. They are perfect in situations where the details matter. If you are not already using repeat backs, consider introducing them as soon as possible. Your future self will thank you.

6. MINIMIZE PRAISE (AND OTHER TOOLS FOR STRONG PERFORMERS)

While praise is wonderfully effective with your strong performers, it's not a good strategy to use with low performers.

Praise sows confusion, sends mixed signals, and misleads your low performer into believing things are okay.

Praise is not the only technique that can cause problems when working with a low performer. Try to avoid (or minimize) all of the following techniques:

• Praise the behaviors you want repeated
• The five-to-one rule
• The expectations activity
• The engagement activity
• Minimize judgment
• Asking permission to give feedback
• The leadership styles of supporting and empowering
• The phrase, "strong performer"

While these are great tools for increasing engagement, motivation, and performance *in strong performers*, they aren't a good choice when working with low performers. They muddy the message and trivialize the consequences of failing to improve.

As the low performer (hopefully) begins to improve their performance, you can cautiously reintroduce these techniques. For example, you can praise specific improvements without diminishing the magnitude of the overall situation:

> "You are making strides in the right direction. You arrived on time every day last week, your reports were turned in on time, and the quality of your work has improved somewhat. Keep that up. Those are the kinds of improvements that will help you get back to being a strong performer as an engineer here at Acme Widgets."

★ ★ ★

Help your low performer truly understand what's going on. It's the best way to help them rise to the challenge of becoming a strong performer.

While you're doing that, you also need to think about the broader organization in which you work.

Chapter 21

Know the Rules

Managing a low performer is serious business. The stakes are high for everyone involved.

So, make sure you know the rules. This means learning your company's policies, coordinating with HR, and being aware of the appropriate laws.

Of course, I don't know who you work for, where you live, or which laws might apply. So we're not going to talk about those specifics. I'm going to assume you will take the time to educate yourself because that's what great managers do.

Instead, I'm going to share three tools that should help no matter where you work.

1. Involve stakeholders.
2. Document, document, document.
3. Learn the performance improvement process (PIP).

1. INVOLVE STAKEHOLDERS

Many people have a stake in what happens with your low performer. You need to keep those stakeholders in the loop early and often. Doing so ensures that you and your employee have access to the right resources. It will also make things easier if you have to take more serious action later on.

If you aren't sure who your stakeholders are, ask your boss or someone from HR. Don't make assumptions. Involving people who don't need to know violates your employee's privacy.

For example, peers of the employee aren't generally told, even when the low performer directly affects them. In my experience, even team leads or project managers are not usually made aware of the situation unless they are also people managers themselves.

2. DOCUMENT, DOCUMENT, DOCUMENT

Managing a low performer can be a legal minefield. There are dozens of ways it can blow up in your face, even if you do everything perfectly.

The emotional, financial, and time costs of legal action can be catastrophic to you, your team, and your company. Even worse, in some locations, the employee can sue the people manager directly.

It's critical that you document all evidence of low performance as soon as possible. Note what you told the employee, when you told them, and possibly, how the employee reacted.

Documentation will help you follow your company's rules as well as make it easier to navigate legal action. Documentation also ends most arguments over minor details, including "he said, she said" debates.

Almost anything counts as documentation—emails, text messages, work products, notes on a notepad, sticky-notes, anything. It doesn't matter *how* you do it, only that you *do* it. Document early, document often. The more, the better.

3. LEARN THE PERFORMANCE IMPROVEMENT PROCESS (PIP)

Many companies have a **performance improvement process (PIP)—a formal process for documenting, tracking, and resolving low performance.** While a full discussion of the PIP is beyond the scope of this book, here are some basics that I wish I had known sooner:

- The word "PIP" refers to both the document and the process.
- The PIP document is formal; it usually includes legal language.
- The PIP document lists behaviors needing improvement.
- The PIP document is often signed by the employee to ensure understanding.
- The PIP document is not a contract—it doesn't prevent you from firing the employee if the situation seriously degrades during the PIP process.
- The PIP process is usually time constrained (e.g., thirty, forty-five or sixty days).
- The PIP process usually ends in one of three ways:

the employee improves to strong-performer status, the employee ends up in a new role/title, or the employee is terminated.

The PIP benefits both the employee and the company. It helps the employee by ensuring they know what to fix and what's at stake. It helps the company by ensuring the manager follows standard protocols, gives employees a chance to succeed, and generates proper documentation.

Also be aware that the PIP is a last-resort intervention. As a people manager, don't delay intervening with a low performer until the problem is so severe it warrants a PIP, hoping your employee will get stronger.

Talk to your employee as soon as you see the warning signs, ensure they know they are becoming a low performer, and help them understand what's at stake.

I've outlined how to make it clear, for the employee's sake. I've made a case for knowing the rules, for the sake of the company. Now, it's time to prepare *yourself*.

Chapter 22

Prepare Yourself

Managing a low performer is one of the hardest parts of being a people manager. You're likely to experience powerful emotions, including sadness, guilt, and anger. And, depending on your company, there will be numerous rules, regulations, and procedures that you're required to follow. Plus, the whole thing can drag on for a long, long time.

It can be overwhelming and lead to a sense of hopelessness.

To stay at the top of your game throughout the whole process—no matter how long it takes—here are four ways to prepare yourself for what you'll need to do while managing a low performer:

1. Adopt a new "forest ranger" schema.
2. Visualize a brighter future.
3. Don't predict the outcome.
4. See the big picture.

1. ADOPT A NEW "FOREST RANGER" SCHEMA

The first way to prepare yourself is to adopt a new schema. Assume the role of a forest ranger, guiding the low performer toward the right (career) path, wherever that may lead.

In this metaphor, the low performer has encountered a rough patch along the path. They might be stuck, turned around, or in need of more resources or information. Or, maybe, they've wandered into an area that is far too difficult for them.

As we discussed earlier, your employee probably doesn't even realize this has happened.

This is where you come in. Use your influence to help guide the employee until they achieve one of two outcomes:

- Get back on track. Sometimes the low performer is both *willing* and *capable* of becoming a strong performer. You make this more likely by doing what a forest ranger would do. Help them understand that they are in a bad place. Then help them find the path, provide missing resources or information, or coach them until they become strong enough to get back on track.
- Find a different path. Sometimes the low performer is either *unwilling* or *incapable* of becoming a strong performer. In that case, they need to find a different path to travel, either in a new role, on a new team, or at an entirely different company. It's your job as the ranger to ensure that happens instead of leaving them lost in the forest.

If you do nothing, the employee remains stuck. They won't

magically wake up one day as a strong performer. Instead, they stagnate, or worse. Meanwhile, your team is suffering from decreased productivity, impaired collaboration, and compromised trust.

Thinking of yourself as a forest ranger will keep you grounded. It reminds you that you're trying to help the employee get to a better place. It keeps you centered, which makes you more effective.

2. VISUALIZE A BRIGHTER FUTURE

Sometimes, managing a low performer can feel like it will never end, particularly if there are complications. If that happens, try to envision the future.

Most scenarios with low performers are resolved within three to six months (depending on your company's processes). While this may seem like a long time, there is light at the end of the tunnel.

Try to be patient with yourself, with the process, and with the company. As the saying goes, "This too shall pass."

3. DON'T PREDICT THE OUTCOME

It's impossible to know how an employee will respond to being told they are a low performer. They might quit, they might try to improve and fail in the end, or they might succeed. They might even rebound spectacularly.

I once had a low performer rebound to become a strong performer, who then became a star performer, who ultimately became critical to my team's success. Anything can happen.

So while you are trying to visualize a brighter future to get through the hard stuff, make sure you are *not* trying to predict the outcome, whether positive or negative.

Predicting the outcome limits your ability to adapt to the actual situation as it unfolds. In addition, it creates a strong bias over everything you see, think, or do. It's an unproductive mental schema that can create self-fulfilling prophecies.

4. SEE THE BIG PICTURE

Try to see the big picture. Remember that a career is a lifelong journey. You are only seeing one part of your employee's journey.

Your low performer is stuck. They are probably unhappy, stressed, or even scared. They certainly aren't experiencing the joy of mastery. By taking action, you are forcing a change. They'll either become a strong performer or find a new path with an appropriate level of difficulty.

The sooner they get unstuck, the faster they can begin making forward progress again. In the grand scheme of their entire career, resolving this situation is in the employee's best interest, even if they have to find a new job somewhere else.

TAKE TIME TO REFLECT

Leadership is a journey, not a destination. Where you are

now is just one step along a path that has no real ending. As you travel that journey, you will experience hard times, like having to manage a low performer.

The goal is to keep striving. Become stronger today than you were yesterday, and stronger tomorrow than you are today. This is part of your leadership journey.

After the situation with your low performer is resolved, self-reflect on your own performance. Ask yourself hard questions like:

- How could I on-board better or improve my hiring criteria?
- What would have made expectations even more clear?
- When could I have provided better feedback?
- How could I have acted sooner?

Look for things you could have done better. Then work to become stronger for next time.

Low performers cause tremendous harm. Watch for the signs. Then use your influence to take action. Ensure your employee understands what's going on, make sure you are following the rules, and prepare yourself for the journey ahead.

Managing a low performer is a long journey. And it's inherently unpredictable. In fact, many things about being a people manager are unpredictable, like the unexpected call I got one Monday morning.

Conclusion

WHAT MAKES GREAT MANAGERS GREAT?

Being a people manager can be wildly unpredictable. One day everything's fine, the next, you're getting a call like this one about my employee, Matt.

> In a flat, almost monotone voice, "This is the Virginia Beach Correctional Facility, calling on behalf of Matt Jones. He gave us your number. Will you accept the call?"
>
> "Uh...what? I mean, Yes! Of course."
>
> A few clicks, then I heard Matt's voice: "Curtiss, can you call my brother? I won't be able to come to work today. They locked me in jail. I need your help."

BECOMING GREAT

Matt trusted me. Your employees should trust you too. They

need you to help them thrive, become engaged, and feel valued.

Don't wait for some future "manager training" to make this happen. Take charge of your leadership journey now by asking the five important questions. Then learn how to answer them.

1. **Expectations:** Use your influence to ensure your employees know what's expected of them. Facilitate the four steps of the expectations activity: brainstorm, organize, shrink, and sacrifice. Reinforce your employees' unique motivations. Figure out what you are trying to accomplish as a leader.

2. **Feedback:** Praise the behaviors you want repeated. See your employees as strong performers. Promote a growth mindset. Choose the right tools for each scenario: confusion, low knowledge/skill, disengagement, low performer, and strong performer.

3. **Psychological safety:** Learn how to listen. Understand that you are threatening. Make it safe to share ideas, ask questions, and make mistakes. Highlight areas of agreement. Ask open-ended questions. Banish "but." "Yes, and..." your employees.

4. **Engagement:** Monitor engagement. Use your influence to increase it where you can. Adopt the right leadership style. Move toward confusion, concern, and conflict.

5. **Low performers:** Recognize the harm. Use formal language to ensure a low performer understands their performance is bad and the potential consequences. Document. Prepare for the long road ahead.

These are the behaviors that make great managers great.

Of course, you don't have to master them all at once. You have the rest of your career. So pick a technique that seems useful. Personally, I recommend starting with one of these three:

1. Run the expectations activity for yourself.
2. Identify three behaviors you will praise among your employees.
3. Banish "but" from your vocabulary.

An easy first step, a medium one, or a hard one—each is powerful.

Whichever technique you start with, take the time to learn how it works. Try it in the real world with your employees. Then refine what you did so you can do it even better next time.

Lead; refine; repeat.

Work to become stronger today than you were yesterday. Then do it again tomorrow and the next day—week after week, month after month. Walk the leadership path until you can look back in awe, realizing that you have become a great manager.

Made in the USA
Las Vegas, NV
16 May 2023

72134822R10125